Home Security

Visit our How To website at **www.howto.co.uk**

At **www.howto.co.uk** you can engage in conversation with our authors – all of whom have 'been there and done that' in their specialist fields. You can get access to special offers and additional content but most imporantly you will be able to engage with, and become a part of, a wide and growing community of people just like yourself.

At **www.howto.co.uk** you'll be able to talk and share tips with people who have similar interests and are facing similar challenges in their lives. People who, just like you, have the desire to change their lives for the better – be it through moving to a new country, starting a new business, growing their own vegetables, or writing a novel.

At **www.howto.co.uk** you'll find the support and encouragement you need to help make your aspirations a reality.

You can go direct to **www.a-z-of-home-security.co.uk** which is part of the main How To site.

How To Books strives to present authentic, inspiring, practical information in their books. Now, when you buy a title from **How To Books**, you get even more than just words on a page.

Home Security

How to keep your home and family safe from crime

D G Conway

howtobooks

Published by How To Books Ltd
Spring Hill House, Spring Hill Road
Begbroke, Oxford OX5 1RX, United Kingdom
Tel: (01865) 375794, Fax: (01865) 379162
info@howtobooks.co.uk
www.howtobooks.co.uk

How To Books greatly reduce the carbon footprint of their books
by sourcing their typesetting and printing in the UK.

British Library Cataloguing in Publication Data
A catalogue record for this book is available from the British Library

ISBN 978 1 84528 403 9

First edition 2005
Reprinted 2005
Second edition 2009
Reprinted 2009
Third edition 2010

Produced for How To Books by Deer Park Productions, Tavistock
Typeset by Kestrel Data, Exeter, Devon
Printed and bound by Bell & Bain Ltd, Glasgow

NOTE: The material contained in this book is set out in good faith for general
guidance and no liability can be accepted for loss or expense incurred as a result
of relying in particular circumstances on statements made in the book. Laws and
regulations are complex and liable to change, and readers should check the current
position with the relevant authorities before making personal arrangements.

Contents

Introduction

Most people know somebody who has been the victim of crime, or they have been a victim themselves. Most people also think that there isn't much they can do to avoid it.

They are wrong! There is a lot that the average person can do to protect themselves, their family and their property. This book will show you how to perform a security review on various different aspects of your home and property, and then take steps to increase your security and avoid crime.

HOW THIS BOOK CAME ABOUT

I have been in the security field for nearly 30 years, serving as a police officer, working in government security and working as a security consultant. I have written this book, based on the knowledge I have gained from that experience, to inform you of the measures you can take to avoid crime.

Generally, statistics show a steady increase in crime, but with some simple facts and information, you can take steps to protect yourself, your family and your property from that crime.

Consider this – half of those who responded to an insurance company survey stated that their greatest worry was that they would be a victim of crime, but they also reported that they had not done anything to protect themselves from the crime they were so worried about, because they didn't think there was anything they could do about it. There was a feeling that 'If it's your turn, then it's going to happen.'

You need to know what you can do to protect yourself. Simple information can help. Did you know, for instance, that a house at the end of a terrace, on a corner, with an alley or a public footpath running down the side or any other public access around it is a lot more likely to be burgled?

Being aware of the threats and taking steps to protect yourself and your property, will make you a lot less likely to become a victim of crime. This book helps you to identify potential vulnerabilities, threats and risks (we will call them all 'problems' from now on), then to propose simple, affordable and achievable countermeasures that the average person can implement to increase their levels of security.

INCREASING YOUR UNDERSTANDING AND KNOWLEDGE

Crime statistics are quite worrying, but they can help us too. Look at these statistics.

- At least 80% of burglars are opportunists; they look for a quick and easy way in and out. Nip next door without locking the front door and your wallet or handbag may be gone when you get back home.

- At least 20% of burglars don't have to force entry, they just walk in through open doors and windows!

- About 60% of burglars enter the target premises from the rear – where there is less chance of them being spotted and/or reported.

- More burglaries happen during the day than at night, when it is quiet and more people are at home to hear and report strange intruders.

Does that worry you? It looks like good news to me, because these statistics tell me how I can best protect my house and belongings by adopting the following countermeasures.

- ✓ By always locking doors and windows and never leaving valuables in a vulnerable place, we deny access to the opportunist thief.

- ✓ By stopping strangers from easily getting to the back of our house by erecting fences and installing lockable side gates, we block the most common access points for burglars.

- ✓ By making sure the house is securely locked during the day, we ensure that it is as safe as it can be, and further reduce the chance of being burgled.

If you adopt those three countermeasures, you have probably made your house at least 70% less likely to become the victim of opportunist theft and domestic burglary – and that's not a bad result considering this is only page 3!

That is the end of lesson one and it doesn't get any harder. Read this book, learning how to identify vulnerabilities, then take steps to remove or reduce the vulnerabilities, and you and your family will be considerably safer. To improve security you need common sense, time to read this book and identify problems, then time to apply countermeasures to resolve them.

To manage the problems you identify I recommend that you take a methodical approach. As you identify and consider any problems, record them with any countermeasures you have identified. The following form shows one method of recording problems and countermeasures, but you are free to use your own method.

Home Security Review, Mr A. Biggins 49 High Street – 29 Feb 200X

PROBLEM
Two gaps in back hedge, behind the garage and at the end of the fence where children break through to collect their balls.

OTHER INFORMATION
Children playing on grass area beside the house have broken through the hedge to retrieve footballs kicked into the garden.

The Council are planting trees and prickly shrubs there to stop children playing and to improve the look of the area – there should be no more ball games there after the end of the month.

COUNTERMEASURES
(a) Dig out the whole hedge and replace it with a six-feet-high chain-link fence.
(b) Plant prickly shrubs among the hedge plants, making sure to fill in the gaps with them.
(c) Leave the hedge as it is but put a chain-link wire fence up on the outside of the hedge.

As you can see, the form records problems, additional information and potential countermeasures. Use a new form to record each problem; this will help you to manage them as you improve your security.

Give each form a title. Identify possible countermeasures yourself or take them from the lists of countermeasures in this book. Using a new form for each problem:

- will give you a record of all problems identified. (Keep these forms safe, and shred them when you have finished with them; they are a burglar's guide to vulnerabilities in your house.)

- allows you to gradually review and refine your understanding of the problems as you research them. The council may have plans to erect a fence along the boundary, which will resolve your problem at no cost or effort to you!

- helps you to understand the problem, and add to and refine the possible countermeasures. If you can't get planning permission for a fence, plant prickly shrubs to repair and reinforce the existing hedge.

- makes it easy for you to review and sort the problems, putting them in priority order. If you only have two problems, one of which is the gaps in the hedge, and the other is that the front door cannot be locked, repairing the front door is a priority and the hedge can wait!

- makes it easy for you to analyse and select the appropriate countermeasures. By crossing out discarded countermeasures you arrive at a record showing the problem and the selected countermeasure(s).

COUNTERMEASURES

(a) ~~Dig out the whole hedge and replace it with a six-feet-high chain-link fence.~~ No planning permission will be given.

(b) Plant prickly shrubs among the hedge plants, making sure to fill in the gaps with them.

(c) ~~Leave the hedge as it is but put a chain-link wire fence up on the outside of the hedge.~~ No planning permission will be given.

Work through this book, reading each section, then review your security. Identify your own vulnerabilities, especially any that may be unique to you and your property. If you live on an island, your unique problem may be an unlocked and readily available motor boat that could be a significant security risk to you.

As you record problems, where you can, identify and record any possible countermeasures at the same time. It is likely that for some problems you may have to leave the countermeasures section blank, coming back to add some when you have had time to think, or you have taken advice from specialists.

IMPLEMENTING COUNTERMEASURES TO YOUR PROBLEMS

When you identify a problem there are basically four things that you can do about that risk:

- Ignore it and hope it goes away.

- Take action to reduce the risk.

- Take action to avoid the risk.

- Take action to remove the risk – by introducing a countermeasure without taking new and unnecessary risks. A countermeasure is something that you can do to improve your security and safety.

My objective is to teach you how to identify problems, and then how to propose and implement appropriate, achievable and affordable countermeasures to increase your security.

Through I provide lists of possible countermeasures, none of the lists is exhaustive; they are simply examples of possible countermeasures. The lists may provide an appropriate countermeasure for your problem, or they may help you to define your own countermeasures.

Suppose the problem you identified is shards of broken glass on the living room couch. The four options are:

- Ignore it – keep using the living room and hope that nobody gets hurt when they sit on the broken glass.

- Reduce the risk – keep using the living room, but warn people not to use the couch because of the broken glass.

- Avoid it – never go into the living room again, so you will not be injured by broken glass.

◼ Remove it – buy and use gardening gloves and goggles to pick up the larger pieces of glass. Use a dustpan to sweep up the smaller pieces. Finally rent a powerful industrial vacuum cleaner to remove the final traces of broken glass before anyone uses the living room again.

Though all options would work, some may be more acceptable and sensible to you and some may seem unrealistic or foolhardy to you, bearing in mind your lifestyle and circumstances.

For most people, the last option, 'removing the risk', will be the most effective long-term solution, even though it requires time, money and effort to achieve it. Knowing your lifestyle and circumstances you are free to adapt the approach to suit your circumstances.

By understanding the problems you face, recognizing the options open to you, and adapting them to your own preferences, you can amend a proposed countermeasure to suit your circumstances. Throughout this book, your primary objectives will be the following.

◼ Recognize problems that exist and how they can affect you and your security.

◼ Look beyond the examples listed, to identify problems appropriate to your unique circumstances.

◼ Study those problems and identify countermeasures that will avoid, remove or reduce them.

■ Compile an action plan, defining the actions you need to take to deliver the selected countermeasure.

■ Continually monitor your life, to recognize any changes that may introduce new problems, requiring you to undertake a new security review to match the changed circumstances.

Though you can use the method to review security for a very close relative, attempting a review for a total stranger will be almost impossible, because you need 'Constant access to, and a close and detailed understanding of, the person and lifestyle of the subject of the review'.

UNDERTAKING A SECURITY REVIEW

This book is broken down into chapters and sections, each one concentrating on a different aspect of your security.

NOTE: While performing a security review you may identify problems that are not security related. Do not ignore them; record them and deal with them in due course.

A security review is completed in simple stages. This book will teach you how to perform each of these stages.

Stage 1 – Review security

Review an aspect of your security to identify and record problems.

Stage 2 – Prioritize problems

Sort and prioritize those problems in order of severity, putting those that present the greatest threat to you and your lifestyle at the top of the list. Concentrate on resolving those problems whose resolution will give you the greatest possible reward for your efforts, while making best use of your limited resources.

Addressing the highest priority problems as soon as possible will enable you to make the greatest improvements to your security.

Stage 3 – Define countermeasures

Identify and define simple, affordable and achievable countermeasures that will resolve the problem to your satisfaction. You may come up with one or more possible countermeasures. If you cannot identify any countermeasures seek help and advice.

Stage 4 – Adopt and prioritize countermeasures

For each problem, consider the possible countermeasures. Look at the options and decide which countermeasure(s) you want to introduce. The considerations include:

- **Benefit** – how much will the proposed countermeasure improve your security? One that delivers marginal benefits should probably be shelved while you concentrate on a countermeasure that will deliver greater benefits.

- **Cost** – identify the financial cost of introducing each countermeasure. Don't forget to look for hidden costs; a new door may cost £325, but the total cost includes a fitting charge of £125, a new lock, letterbox, handles etc. which cost a further £75, and repairing plaster and paint around the door which will cost a further £55.

■ **Resources** – perhaps you can do the work yourself. If not, get at least three independent quotes, accepting the quote that offers best value. Remember, that may not necessarily be the cheapest quote! Factors such as the tradesman's reputation, any personal recommendations you may have, the quality of the work proposed, the tradesman's availability, and more should also be considered. Don't forget your 'gut feelings'; if something seems not quite right about them, use someone else.

■ **Degree of risk** – you should also consider the level of risk you will be taking by not introducing a countermeasure. Not fixing the lock on the front door leaves the house totally insecure – a major risk which should be considered when you are deciding what countermeasures to take.

Stage 5 – Implement

When your review has been made, and you have decided which countermeasures to implement, in what order of priority – do it. This is the most vital stage of the process, the time when you act to protect yourself against the problems you have identified.

PACING YOUR REVIEW

Don't rush it, but don't delay unnecessarily. Read this book carefully and think about each area discussed. When you fully understand it you should have a valuable insight into the way apparently inconsequential and innocent acts, omissions and decisions could put your security at risk.

Using the information in this book, you will be able to identify and prioritize the specific problems that could turn you into a victim. More importantly, you will have learned to look at every-day situations and be able to identify where new risks and threats lie, allowing you to take immediate steps to avoid them. You will then be able to make changes to increase your security, by continually reviewing your life, identifying and avoiding new threats as they occur.

WHAT YOU WILL NEED

To understand and be able to perform an effective security review, you need this book, and:

- time to read the book and consider the range and type of problems discussed, then time to think through and identify how any of the issues raised could affect your unique lifestyle;

- the ability to decide on the relevance to your house and lifestyle of the problems discussed, while taking a broader view to decide if you are subject to other, more specific and unique, threats and risks;

■   forms, or other means of recording problems as you discover them, as well as for assigning appropriate and possible countermeasures;

■   the skill, finances and resources to implement any countermeasure that you select.

The skills and knowledge required to perform a security review include:

■   accepting that there are threats and risks all around us;

■   accepting that some of your activities make you more vulnerable, and hence at a greater risk of becoming a victim;

■   an ability to learn how to identify potential threats and risks in 'your world';

■   an ability to learn how to identify possible countermeasures to reduce or remove your exposure to those threats and risks;

■   an ability to remain alert to your surroundings, particularly in relation to some of your activities and actions;

■   an ability to become equally aware of the activities and behaviour of the people around you, and to be prepared to take action to avoid developing or potential risks.

WHEN TO CARRY OUT YOUR REVIEW

As soon as possible, if you have never performed a security review.

During the year you should remain alert to changing circumstances and possible new problems, but you should perform a formal lifestyle security review every 12 months.

If there is a significant change in your life, you should at least undertake a partial security review. The more significant the change, the more reason there is to perform a complete security review! Reasons include:

- moving house;

- starting a new job;

- taking a different mode of transport to work – for example, the train instead of driving;

- getting married;

- having a child;

- coming into some money.

It's your decision!

It is important to remember that this is general advice. Laws change and people and their lifestyles differ. Your lifestyle may be eccentric or unusual. You may have strange allergies, a love for dangerous sports and a pet tiger! Because there is only one 'you', this book can only raise your level of awareness and offer general advice, and you must treat it as such.

You must decide if you want to act on any of this advice.

You must select and implement actions appropriate to you and your lifestyle.

You must check with relevant experts to make sure that you do the right thing for your circumstances.

2

Undertaking a House Security Review

You may live in a house, flat, maisonette, detached mansion, cottage, villa, mobile home or terrace. This chapter explains how to review and improve the security of the place where you live; for simplicity we'll call it your 'house'.

Your house is a critical element in your safety and security for many reasons, including the following.

- Most people are at home for upwards of ten hours every day.

- You expect your house to be safe, so you probably let your guard down when you are there.

- For around eight hours each day most people are in bed asleep, and therefore particularly vulnerable.

- You rely on your house to shelter your loved ones and keep them safe.

- Your house is usually your biggest investment.

- You use your house to store all of your possessions, even when you are not at home.

Using common sense and knowledge, you can take steps that will make your house as safe as it can be without turning it into a fortress or a prison.

NOTE: Shared accommodation, student digs, a detached house and a tenth-storey flat all present unique problems, but they also share some common elements. They all have access points, neighbours, doors and windows, approaches and a perimeter. Surveying the security of a detached house which has gardens, garages, outbuildings and sheds is considerably more complicated than surveying a flat because for a flat you can usually ignore the process that relates to fences, gardens, sheds and other outbuildings.

In this book I will therefore describe the process necessary to complete the most complicated review, and that is for a semi-detached two-storey house with a garden, neighbours, garage, greenhouse, shed, easy access via ground-floor doors and windows, potential access to first-floor windows, and flat roofs etc. In comparison, completing a survey on a tenth-floor flat would be easy.

No matter what type of building you call home, when you have read and understood each chapter, you should apply the approach to your unique accommodation.

When you have learned how to do this, you could also use some elements of this security review method to review the security of a property you are considering buying or renting. As you will not have free access to that property, you will not be able to perform some elements as thoroughly, but a review will still give you an impression of the security of that property.

The following advice will enable you to perform a security review in order to address and improve security and reduce threats and risks to your house.

RESEARCHING YOUR AREA

Step one in surveying your current house is to research crime statistics for the area. This will help you to decide which problems are most important and should be addressed first.

When buying a house most people check to see if a motorway is being built at the bottom of the garden, but few people check on the security aspects of a house. Yet the information you uncover may be critical to your decision to buy that house or not.

I have listed a number of sources of information that are available to you to start you off. Research is of most value for a property and area you are thinking of moving to.

Take a look yourself

Going to take a look yourself is the best option. Local taxi drivers are also a good source of information; they quite freely say if they think an area is safe after dark, or somewhere they would like to live.

Estate agents

Local estate agents know the status of an area. Try an open question, 'I'm thinking of buying a house in Forest Park. What's that like for crime?' It's their job to sell houses, but they should be able to tell you what different areas are like. If several estate agents tell you it would be safer to move to a war zone, look elsewhere.

Local people

Ask around the area, carefully. Local shops and shopkeepers are good sources of information. If the shops are fitted with CCTV cameras, steel shutters and bullet-proof glass, you know that trouble is not very far away!

Talk to shopkeepers and older residents. Don't ask leading questions, try a more neutral approach, such as 'Has it changed much around here?' That tends to get a more balanced response, and gives you an opportunity to nudge the conversation towards crime and safety. They may say, 'It used to be quiet, until that nightclub opened. We haven't had a decent night's sleep for nearly two years.'

What they say is another element of evidence to enable you to build your picture of crime levels in the area.

Insurance companies

Insurance companies pay out on claims for crime and damage, so they know which areas have a higher crime rate. Ask about crime in a given area, or do a comparison. Ask for a quote to insure a house of a similar size and value to your current house but in the area you are interested in. If your current insurance premium is £295, and a quote for a similar house in the new area is £875, the risk must be a lot higher there. Talk to the insurance company or agent, and ask why.

Local authorities

Local authority staff are worth talking to. Try dropping into a café or pub used by council staff. They know where they have to repair damage caused by vandals, where problem families live, and where they won't go alone. Be honest and ask them outright for reports about different areas.

Local newspapers

Buy the local newspapers for a few weeks or look through back issues in the local library. They carry the sort of information you need on muggings, robberies, burglaries, car crime, assaults etc. Information from local papers can also give you an idea of crime trends; over the years you might see a reduction in vandalism and an increase in street robbery and burglary.

Schools

The local school will be aware of trends in youth crime because they deal with it on a daily basis. If you have children, you will want to know what the schools in the area are like anyway. So when you visit them, extend your questioning to crime in the local community and their perception of different areas.

Local community police officer

What you would like the local police officer to say is 'Don't move into that road – the whole family at number 27 are criminals and there is a drug dealer living in number 34.' There are legal issues that prevent his being able to speak so openly, but you could try talking to the local community police officer. I would be quite open and say, 'I know you can't give me details, but I am wondering what the crime is like in that area of town because I am thinking of buying a house in Badger Road. Would you buy one there?' If he replies, 'I would never buy a house in Badger Road,' you can draw your own conclusions from that.

Environment agency

In most areas you should check with the environment agency to make sure that the house you are looking at is not at risk of flooding. On the environment agency website www.environment-agency.gov.uk you can type in a postcode and check flooding maps. This will give you a good idea of the risk of flooding for any given location and property.

Internet sources

Various other Internet sources are available for you to make your checks as well. Some local authorities and other organizations hold information about crime rates and trends. For example, www.crimestatistics.org.uk holds information that you can search on a postcode basis.

No matter how good the house looks, the information you have uncovered above may make you decide to look elsewhere. You went to a great deal of trouble to find this information, so use it!

PERFORMING A HOUSE SECURITY SURVEY

The most important thing you can do if you want to improve the security and safety of your house is to perform a security survey on your house.

- If you are proposing to undertake a security review of your own house, go ahead immediately and survey it.

- If you are proposing to review security for a house owned by a close relative, don't try it until you have had some practice reviewing your own house.

- If you are thinking of undertaking a security survey on a house you are considering of buying:
  - don't try it until you have had some practice reviewing your own house;
  - accept that you will not have full and free access, so you will be unable to perform a full security survey.

CARRYING OUT AN EXTERNAL SECURITY SURVEY

Don't try to use this method until you have read and understood the information in this book. Read each section thoroughly, then with a pen handy to record your findings, go ahead.

Your first task is to undertake an external security survey of the area around the house, the garden and the close perimeter of the house. No matter where you live, the procedure is the same, but circumstances may change the content and scope of the external survey.

If you live in a 15th-floor flat you probably don't need to look at fences and garden sheds, but there may be other issues to consider, such as a cycle cupboard on the landing outside each flat.

The main objective of an external survey is to stand back and take a look at the house and the immediate surroundings. Record any problems as you identify them, taking a few minutes to consider and list any possible countermeasures. The example countermeasures listed below will help you to think along the right lines, but never forget that you have a unique lifestyle so you are the best person to recognize appropriate problems and to identify appropriate, affordable, justifiable and achievable countermeasures.

Area

Walk around the surrounding roads and make a note of your general impression. Is it 'general light industrial units with some residential', 'run-down shabby residential', or maybe 'affluent commuter belt'?

That is the impression that the rest of the world receives when they approach your house, and gives useful pointers in relation to the security of your house. For example, though the interpretations are rather stereotyped, different appearances could mean different things:

Industrial could mean lots of people around from 9 a.m. to 6 p.m. Mondays to Fridays, but deserted after 6 p.m. and at weekends and bank holidays, making life easier for burglars in the quiet hours.

Shabby residential could mean a community in decline, with high unemployment and no community pride, and where crime and vandalism are commonplace. This is only one interpretation though – it could just as easily reflect the recent closure of a major employer, bad budgetary management and incompetence by the local authority, or it could hide an up-and-coming area where property values are set to shoot through the roof.

Be careful what you say; don't offend or upset people by asking too many questions. Aim to be conversational and wait until later to write down what they tell you.

Affluent commuter belt means large, well-kept, expensive houses with wealthy residents – but think like a criminal, this could mean a lot of valuable possessions, husband away at work 8 a.m. until 6 p.m. each weekday, wife at home when the Mercedes is there. It's worth checking to see when they come and go. Even the garden can be profitable; a ride-on mower may be worth up to £5,000, and specimen carp from the pond can cost up to £3,000 each. The large and mature garden offers plenty of cover for a burglar. Mr and Mrs Big-House probably take at least two holidays a year, which equals four weeks when nobody is at home. It's worth coming back with a van for that garden equipment – if anyone asks, 'We're taking it for service.' The downside is, it's probably alarmed!

New starter homes means young residents starting out on the property ladder. Probably both out at work, though mum might be at home with a new baby. Young and trendy, so they have the latest electronic goods; should be worth breaking in. The downside is that starter homes are packed closely together, with small gardens, no mature plants and hedges, so criminal activity would be easily heard or spotted.

Rural could mean a mixture: some smaller homes, worth taking a look at for money and portable valuables; some large country houses packed with antiques. Most large homes have an alarm, but some don't. If an alarm sounds, it will take the police at least five minutes to reach the property, which is why they use silent alarms. Rural properties often have outbuildings, offering a range of easily accessible valuables, from garden machines to vehicles, expensive horse tack (e.g. saddles and bridles) to sporting equipment (e.g. skis and fishing equipment), and pedigree animals to tool-boxes. Little passing traffic and no close neighbours are a huge benefit to a burglar.

Look for signal crime. Look out for vandalism, fly-tipping, graffiti, broken glass and other petty crime. This is called 'signal crime', it is a signal of criminal activity in the area, possible lack of community pride and unwillingness to speak out to prevent crime. Generally, where there is visible crime there will inevitably be more serious crime that is not apparent to a casual observer, and usually crime breeds crime.

Who is around? You should be looking to see who is moving around the area. Criminals don't wear badges but you get a feel for the type and numbers of people who move around. Just as people mature, communities tend to mature as well.

The pattern of movement on new estates may be that each weekday dad leaves for work, then mum and the kids leave to go to school, later mum comes home alone and the cycle reverses itself after three in the afternoon. Twenty years later, with the kids at university, the pattern of movement in that community will change radically. Eventually it reaches a stage when the residents are all retired and there is no pattern of movement. They all come and go as they want to, because they no longer have regular commitments to meet.

Checking on who is around at different times will identify periods of greater risk to you and your property. In the young community your house will be fairly safe between eight-thirty and say ten in the morning because there are too many people moving around. Criminals don't want to be seen and reported so they will not generally be active during that time.

If you live near the local football stadium you might find that there is a peak in crimes after the match on a Saturday, when drunken louts spill out of the stadium in unsociably high spirits, vandalizing cars and gardens and assaulting people as they move towards the railway station to go home.

Drunken louts – countermeasures I
✓   Use common sense and avoid the risk. Park your car elsewhere on a Saturday, lock your gate, don't go out when the match is finishing and don't leave anything valuable in the front garden.

✓   If crimes peak after each football match, report it and demand that something should be done. Get the local residents together and record everything as evidence to support your claim. Write to the football club, the local police and local authority, copying the complaint to your local MP. Support that complaint with a petition from residents and a list of evidence.

You may be subjected to regular crime if perhaps you live on a route that is used by drunks leaving a poorly managed public house at the end of your dead-end street. They all have to pass your house to get to and from the pub and at closing time the landlord throws them out in high spirits. In such circumstances it is common for residents to be plagued by petty crime and disturbance almost every evening.

Drunken louts – countermeasures 2

✓   In those circumstances residents should make a log of all incidents and any calls made to the police and their response. With a few months' worth of recorded evidence I would then make a formal complaint to the police, the landlord and the local licensing authority and copy it all to my MP.

Identifying patterns of movement and the type of people moving around at different times will help you to accurately assess threats and risks in a given area.

Approaches to your house

A house on a straight road that runs north to south has two approaches – from the north and from the south – while a house on a crossroads with a footpath running across the fields behind it has multiple approaches. You should check each approach to your house.

Walk around and review *all* approaches to your house to perform a thorough security review. For each approach use your 'criminal's eye'; try to identify any actual or possible vulnerabilities. From the bus stop opposite a burglar may get an inviting view of your new 50-inch plasma TV, and laptop computer in the lounge. Other things to look out for include:

- easy entry points and easy exit carrying your valuables;

- low or broken fences and any cover offered by shrubs etc;

- unlocked sheds containing expensive tools and equipment;

- insecure workshops and garages, allowing burglars to take an inventory of what they can steal or use to break into your house;

- expensive statues, specimen carp, mountain bikes and other valuables in the garden;

- greenhouses with expensive propagators and heaters;

- garden tools (spade or fork) that can be used to force a window or door;

- ladders left outside which will give easy access to roofs and windows;

- any signs of a dog, or a burglar alarm;

▧ any signs that the resident is disabled or elderly, such as wheelchair ramps and handrails;

▧ any vehicles associated with the premises.

Vehicles can tell us a lot about the residents of a particular property. An electrician's transit van and a Ford Focus parked outside a house indicate that the owner is an electrician (he will be out Mondays to Fridays from 9 a.m. to 5 p.m.). The van contains valuable tools and equipment and there is an interesting-looking locked shed or workshop. Mrs Electrician drives the Focus and, having seen a baby seat in the car, they have a baby!

A burglar can read your property as easily as that. As he passes by he will read all of this and more. That is why you have to identify and review all approaches to your house, so that you know what he can see.

Add complications like a garage forecourt beside a property and a public playing field at the rear and the review becomes more difficult. No matter what the state of your property, check all approaches and make sure you know what is visible.

Is anyone in?

Criminals don't want to be disturbed or caught, so may prefer to carry out their crimes in or on empty premises. If a house looks occupied most criminals will walk past and look for an easier target. They don't need to take risks when there are so many more vulnerable houses just up the road. There are about 28 million dwellings in the UK so the burglar has plenty of choice!

Your objective is to take as many steps to protect yourself as are reasonable and you can justify. With each step, you make your house that little bit harder for burglars to target and give them that much more encouragement to move on to easier targets up the road.

At night, a house with no lights on, an open gate and garage door with no car visible, is almost certainly empty, and an empty house is an easy target. Even without those clues, it is amazingly easy to find out if there is anyone at home – just knock at the door!

If nobody answers there is probably nobody at home, so burglars can slip around to the back and help themselves. If somebody does answer the door, the criminal excuses himself by saying something like 'Does Jack the mechanic live here?' You say no and close the door, and the burglar walks away because there are a lot more vulnerable houses down the road.

Helpful neighbours have even unwittingly helped criminals. A neighbour saw somebody knocking next door and 'helpfully' informed the person that 'Mr and Mrs Jones are in Brighton visiting their daughter, they won't be back until Tuesday.' Guess what Mr and Mrs Jones discovered when they got back on Tuesday?

Empty house – countermeasures

✓   Tell a friendly and trustworthy neighbour that you are going to be away.

✓   Consider leaving a contact number with them in case of problems.

✓   If you will be away a few days consider leaving the number of a nearby relative who will be able to act as key holder if the neighbour thinks there is a problem.

Finding your house

How hard is it for the emergency services to find your house, at night and in the rain? If the houses are numbered, it is quite easy, but if your house is identified by a name only, it might not be so easy. To find 'Woodpeckers' in Badger Road the emergency services may have to drive the length of the road, stopping to check the name of every house – if the house has a nameplate visible from the road. If the house owner makes it difficult by not erecting or maintaining a nameplate, emergency response will be delayed.

To check how hard your house is to find, ask somebody who isn't familiar with it to find it at night in the rain. See how long it takes them, and don't cheat by putting all the lights on or standing at the front door.

Finding your house – countermeasures

✓   If possible, ask your neighbours to number houses in the road in sequence, making it easy to find each house.

✓   If houses have names only, ensure that the house names are clearly marked, visible and easy to read.

✓   Get everyone in the road to standardize nameplate styles and locations to help identify properties.

✓ If you have to call the emergency services, give further guidance, such as 'From Fox Lane, turn into Badger Road; "Woodpeckers" is the first house on the right after the wooden bus shelter.'

✓ If emergency services have been called and it is safe to do so, send somebody out into the road to attract the attention of the driver. Do tell the operator of your intentions, so that this information can be passed on to the driver of the emergency vehicle, who will then be warned to look out for you.

Front view of your house

At the front gate, stop and take note of what a criminal might see, such as:

- unlocked or open garages, sheds, greenhouses and other outbuildings;

- open windows and doors in the main house;

- ladders left out;

- flat roofs with easy access to second-floor windows (upper-floor windows are almost always less secure than ground-floor windows);

- vehicles;

- signs of dogs (not welcome);

- indications of burglar alarms such as bell boxes or signs;

- visible signs of goods worth stealing, such as televisions, computers, etc.;

■ indications of lifestyle patterns (e.g., a works van means he is out to work all day, children's toys could mean mum does school or playgroup runs each day).

Below is a ready-made list of simple, effective and free or inexpensive countermeasures you can take to increase security, based on the examples from the list above.

Front view – countermeasures

✓ Always lock garages, sheds, greenhouses and other outbuildings.

✓ When you are going out make sure that all windows and doors are locked.

✓ Remove and securely store ladders and other tools and equipment that could be stolen or used by criminals.

✓ Secure access to flat roofs, making sure that second-floor windows accessible from flat roofs are as secure as they can be while still allowing you to escape in an emergency.

✓ Make vehicles as secure as you can. Put the car in the garage and shut the doors, even if you are going out later the same day. Make it harder for the criminal to 'read' your property. When you do go out leave some lights on in the house and leave a radio tuned to a talk station. Anyone listening will hear only voices and, hopefully, will assume people are inside talking, so they will move on.

✓ Put up a 'beware of the dog' sign, or leave some dog toys on the patio even if you don't have a dog.

✓   If you can afford it, invest in a burglar alarm that is monitored 24 hours a day. The monitoring service will call the police if the alarm is triggered. You can also buy dummy alarm boxes and dummy CCTV cameras to try to fool criminals into thinking your security is better than it is. They may fool the opportunist thief, but they won't fool the career criminal.

✓   Blinds or curtains at windows will reduce visibility for criminals. If they can't easily see who or what is inside they will probably move on.

✓   You cannot easily hide some lifestyle indicators, such as a works van in the drive or the school runs, but you can deliberately break patterns sometimes. Leave the van at home occasionally and take the car to work if you are training or have a day of meetings. Co-operate with other parents so that sometimes you all collect each other's children too, or ask Granny or Grandpa to sit at home and be deliberately visible while you are out taking or collecting the children.

By removing indications of vulnerability, and introducing as many anti-crime measures as you can, you make your house a less tempting target, giving the criminal more reason to walk on to find an easier target.

Frontal access

Look at frontal access to your house. Criminals have been known to bring a removal lorry and clear a house of anything of value, or drive up in daylight and load an expensive car on to a breakdown truck and drive off with it, claiming they were taking it for repair. Reducing access makes any property more secure, but bear in mind the following considerations.

■ Planning consent – check to see what you are allowed to do.

■ Ease of access – this is needed for genuine visitors, deliveries and emergency services.

■ Aesthetics – even if you get planning permission for a high wire fence, will the neighbours object, and will you like living in what looks like a prison camp?

■ Cost – will the cost of the measures you are considering be justified by the increase in the levels of security and peace of mind you will get from the work?

■ Value – can you justify the cost of the work against the value of the premises? If your cottage is valued at £200,000, is it sensible to spend £300,000 making it more secure? You would be better off selling up and combining what you get for your property with what you were thinking of spending to make it secure. That way you can buy a new house that is already more secure.

Frontal access – countermeasures

✓ Erecting fences and locking side gates will deny criminals easy access to the rear of your property.

✓ Locking the gates to the drive will prevent anyone from easily taking a vehicle in or out of the premises without your permission.

✓ Siting the pedestrian gate under a street lamp and removing bushes and hedges at the front of your property gives passing traffic a clear view of activity in the front of your house, making it a lot more secure.

✓   Depending on the location and conditions of your property, consider installing lighting that may be operated by a switch, timer or automatically triggered by movement sensors. Criminals will not want to be floodlit while they try to attack your property.

Boundary lines

Boundary lines may be marked with fences, hedges, walls or, on open-plan estates, nothing. Check the boundary of your property, noting any problems.

The general rule is to protect the rear of the property with strong boundaries. This stops criminals getting in easily, making them less likely to target your house.

At the front of your house, try to make intruders visible to neighbours and passing traffic. Your property is safer if anyone passing has an uninterrupted view of the front of the property, as it makes it less likely that a criminal will try to scale the fence or side gate to get to the back.

Some fences and barriers may need planning permission, so check before you do anything. You also have a duty of care and should not allow or cause harm to anyone on your property, whether they are legitimate visitors or not (Occupiers Liability Act 1984).

Walls Brick, block or concrete walls are solid, but they can give criminals good foot and hand holds, allowing them to climb over safely. Once inside, they are also shielded from the outside world, hence the advice to have clear views of the front of your property.

Simple walls may stop an opportunist thief, because they want to be in and out quickly and easily and a wall or fence will slow them down. Expensive burglar alarms, approved and legal anti-climbing paint and spikes etc. can deter even the dedicated burglar.

Wooden fences Prices vary. Of variable strength, but not as strong as a wall – you get what you pay for. Wooden fences may be cheaper than walls, but require more maintenance effort and they can be climbed. One flaw is that criminals can kick or cut a hole in even the strongest wooden fence.

Wire fences Available in a variety of heights and styles, these can be inexpensive. The can be alarmed, but that is an expensive option. A wire fence will deter opportunists, especially if it is topped with barbed wire. It is possible to scrape a hollow under the wire and slide through, so there is an option to have them installed with buried 'aprons' – concrete footings and stakes set into the ground – but that makes them a lot more expensive.

Their ultimate flaw is that anyone with a cheap pair of wire cutters in their pocket can get in, and a vertical slice cut through the wire behind a bush or tree, can remain undiscovered for weeks.

Metal railings These are expensive to very expensive. Spiked railings are probably the most secure common fencing there is. Foundations and aprons block easy access underneath. A hacksaw and plenty of time, or a noisy mechanical cutter is needed to cut through railings, and a hole in metal railings is easily spotted.

Alarms and sensors can be fitted for added protection as an expensive option.

Hedges Natural in appearance, these make the home feel less like a prison. Cheap, decorative and ineffective, up to expensive and impenetrable, they prevent casual intrusion. The right plants, together with correct watering and pruning, will produce a dense and almost impenetrable barrier. However, drought and disease can destroy a hedge in weeks; fire can destroy it in minutes. An intruder with pruning shears can cut a hole in minutes. Hedges take months or years to reach maturity. The cost of maintenance is high, and the protection offered is variable. Prickly plants offer better all-round protection, but you may decide against them if you have children.

Open-plan This style is a legal requirement on some properties, aesthetically pleasing to many and uncomfortably exposed to some. Boundary lines may be marked by 'marker posts', but there is no barrier between properties or between public and private areas. Some deeds and tenancy agreements specify that boundaries must be erected and maintained, while others specify no boundary. Security against intrusion is non-existent, but the open-plan nature does mean that a criminal will be totally exposed as they creep around a property.

Boundary lines – countermeasures

✓ Combining boundary styles will increase security. A chain-link fence with a prickly hedge planted inside works well. The fence prevents casual intruders, and the prickly bushes deter more persistent intruders. With a combination barrier, the hedge does not have to be so expensive or carefully tended, because the chain-link fence is the primary barrier, and hedge roots stop intruders digging under the fence.

✓ Insubstantial trellis is an inexpensive countermeasure. Putting a trellis on top of an existing fence or wall is a major deterrent, cheap to buy and fairly easy to install. It deters intruders because they know that if they try to climb over a barrier and trellis, the trellis will break, making noise, disturbance, and maybe injuring them.

✓ Add noise-makers. For modest cost add alarms or noise-makers to a boundary. Attach bells, or tins containing a handful of gravel, to thin lines and stretch them along the barrier. If an intruder tries to climb the wall he will pull the line and make a noise. *NOTE*: 'traps' designed and set to injure intruders are illegal and using them could put you in court or even prison.

✓ Security patrols. You could pay a security company to patrol your property. A variety of services are available at a range of costs.

✓ Cheat. Erect signs saying 'Beware – Guard Dog' or 'Premises Patrolled By XYZ Security'. A motivated professional burglar may not be put off, but a passing opportunist thief might be.

Gates

Fences almost always have to have at least one gate built into them. The fence then becomes as secure as the gate that has been installed. Gates should be more secure than the fence, while being simple and convenient for authorized people to unlock them, open, use and then secure them again afterwards.

Because a gate is designed to allow access through a barrier, it is a weak point in that barrier.

Gates – countermeasures

✓ Don't install a gate unless it is absolutely necessary.

✓ The smaller the opening in the barrier and smaller the gate, the more secure the barrier will be.

✓ Gate posts and frames should be stronger than the surrounding fence posts, because they have to take additional strain during opening and closing and from knocks while in use.

✓ Hinges should be secured to prevent intruders simply lifting a gate off its hinges.

✓ Gate locks should be as solid and secure as locks on a door, preferably with a two-point locking system to distribute the load and stress on the gate and gate post.

Paths

The positioning and construction of footpaths can add to or detract from security. Nobody can walk on a gravel path without making a noise. Therefore a gravel drive and path surrounding your house acts like a mediaeval moat, stopping intruders from creeping up to the house.

Remember, you don't have to adopt all possible countermeasures immediately. Keep that information in mind and choose a house with a gravel path next time you move, or install one when you remodel the garden.

Feel of the property

Now you have finished the external review, what is your feel for the property? The following examples illustrate what I mean by this.

Open house. A criminal's delight! Quiet road, no passing traffic, windows left open and a spare front door key under the doormat. Family members carelessly, leave the front door unlocked and open. Cars are left with valuables in clear sight and keys in the ignition. Gates are open, there are overgrown shrubs and bushes in the garden, and broken fences leave a dozen ways in and out. Valuables are easily visible from the street, there are no pets, no alarm and apparently the occupants have no idea of how to protect themselves or their property.

Fortress. Strong secure fences and prickly shrubs. High, locked side gates leave no access to the rear. Two German Shepherd dogs are loose inside the house and back garden. The house is alarmed, with windows and doors clearly protected by professionally installed locks. There are gravel paths and drive, with sensor-operated flood lighting. No valuables are visible from the street. This is a house where the residents are obviously security conscious.

If you were a criminal, which house would you target? More importantly, on a scale of 'open house' to 'fortress', where do you think your property stands?

Carry on with your survey, keeping your impression of the property in mind. If your house is more open house than fortress, criminals will be taking a greater interest in it. You will have to work harder to bring it closer to the fortress assessment. Now that you have begun to identify them, implement the countermeasures as soon as you can, such as locking the ladder away, locking the garage door and closing the house windows.

Back garden

Check the side and back fences. What state are they in? What's on the other side? Are the fences easy to climb? Can intruders get into your back garden across fields, allotments or via neighbouring gardens?

Are there unruly bushes and wild plants in which a criminal could hide unseen? What work needs doing to make the garden a safer and more secure environment? Make a note of countermeasures you could take.

Back garden – countermeasures

- ✓ Repair or replace broken or rotten fences.

- ✓ Plant prickly hedges as a secondary barrier.

- ✓ Cut down or trim unruly shrubs and bushes to remove hiding places that a criminal could use.

- ✓ Trim back any overhanging trees that may help a criminal to climb over fences.

- ✓ Lock away any ladders, tools, planks of wood or anything else that a criminal could use to enter your property.

- ✓ Consider installing sensor-operated floodlights.

Children's bikes and toys

The value of children's bikes and toys left around the house can be considerable. No matter what it is, you should not leave hundreds of pounds' worth of property unprotected in your garden.

Outbuildings

For complete security, you should review and secure outbuildings.

Garages Assess vulnerability. What's it built of? Bricks or concrete are quite secure, but wooden planks rot or can be cut through or prised off in minutes. Are any windows out of sight at the back? Could somebody climb through? How secure are the doors? What locks are used and with how many locking points? (A three-point locking system offers better security.)

Can people see inside? Is there anything worth stealing? Check and add up the estimated replacement value of what you can see – the total will probably surprise you.

You should have a record (see example below) of the make, model and serial number of all tools, bicycles etc. that are kept in the garage, plus a photograph if possible. For further information, see the section 'Recording the details of your house contents' later in the chapter.

Description	Make	Model	Serial Number	Unique Marks	Other Information	Photograph
Hammer Drill	Black & Decker	AA34/Iv	BD-63859FN	Postcode engraved on case and handle	Chuck key tied to cable with red plastic string	Video of garage contents
Mechanics Tool Case	Banner & Jones	Set 456.78	546-4A44	Postcode engraved in case and on some hand tools		Photo Album 2, pictures 2 and 3
Gent's Mountain Bike	Mountain Trail	Pro Rider 3	MT-PR3-365498697	Postcode engraved on bottom of crossbar	Mostly electric blue, red flashes on crossbar and sprung forks	Photo Album I, Pictures 6 and 7

Make a note of any problems you find, with appropriate countermeasures.

Sheds Survey sheds as well, estimating the value of the contents, and recording details of valuable items and weaknesses.

Greenhouses Even greenhouses can contain valuable equipment, or be used to store bikes and other items in winter. Do the same checks on the greenhouse.

Outbuildings – countermeasures

✓   Check construction and maintenance. Locking the door when the back wall is rotten is a waste of time. Note any problems and countermeasures.

✓ Always lock and secure all outbuildings.

✓ Make sure all locks are effective and secure.

✓ Note the value, make, model and serial number of each item.

✓ Mark all valuables with your postcode and house number. If you do mark your property, display a 'Marked Property' sign at the front door of your house and on the shed, greenhouse and garage doors.

✓ A photograph showing a scale in the picture (such as a tape measure or ruler) will be of help to identify your property if it is lost or stolen.

CARRYING OUT A CLOSE PERIMETER SURVEY

Perform the close perimeter survey when the house is locked and secured exactly as you secure it when you go out. Walk around the house within about arm's reach of it, looking at potential access points and other problems. Consider the following points when you are looking out for problems.

▪ Criminals prefer to use doors, so pay attention to them. Check and note their strength, fit and locks. Have keys been left inside door locks? If so, breaking the glass will give the intruder easy access to that door.

▪ Drainpipes and service cables may allow intruders to climb in through upper-storey windows.

▪ Solid trellis and climbing plants may allow intruders to climb to windows, balconies or a flat roof.

- Inspect all windows from the outside. Check and note their strength, fit and locks. Have window keys been left inside the locks? Laminated or wired glass may be beneficial in hidden corners.

- Check for hidden corners where plants or outbuildings could allow an intruder to wait or work unobserved.

- Check the state of the brickwork, tiles and cladding; if they are badly maintained this could make it easy for a criminal to gain access.

- Check for any access to roof areas, which could in turn give easy access to less secure windows on upper floors.

- Check for access to roofs. I once attended a house where intruders had climbed from a fence on to the roof of the house, lifted a few tiles and dropped into the house through the roof! (Fit a lock to the loft door.)

- Walk around any outbuildings, including garages and stables etc. performing a similar review on them.

- Check any exterior lighting. What area does it cover and how is it operated? *NOTE*: in a remote property with no neighbours to see intruders, automatic lights offer little benefit other than helping an intruder to see what he is doing. Lights are generally only effective where people are at home, or where neighbours and passing traffic can see any criminal activity.

You may well discover some threats that are not security related, such as loose electrical wiring in the greenhouse. Record them and deal with them appropriately. Always check for landlord or planning permission or other restrictions on your countermeasures.

Close perimeter – countermeasures

✓ Drainpipes and cables. Replace metal pipes with reproduction plastic ones as long as your landlord and council will allow you to. They are functional, but will not support the weight of a climbing intruder.

✓ Trellis and climbing plants. Make sure that the trellis or climbing plants on your walls is too weak to support an intruder. Climbing plants damage brickwork anyway and can promote and support damp and pests.

✓ Door and window locks. Are they secure? Without damaging them, give them a push or pull. Could you force them if you wanted to? Feel for any movement, loose locks or frames, note problems and resolve them. Never leave windows open when you are out. They are an invitation to burglars.

✓ Hidden corners. Identify access points that are hidden from view. You could fit metal bars on windows in hidden corners, or cut back bushes so that they are not hidden.

✓ Brickwork. Rotten brickwork can make a home vulnerable. It has been known for a criminal to easily chip a hole in a rotten brick wall to gain access to premises.

✓ Flat roof access. A flat roof will give easy access to upper floors. Upper-floor windows are often less secure than ground-floor windows so make them secure.

✓ First-floor roof access. Deny access: hide ladders etc., use anti-climbing paint, anti-intrusion spikes, install weak plastic drainpipes, plant prickly plants around the walls.

✓ Outbuildings. Secure them to protect valuable contents, and prevent access to tools that could be used to break into your property.

✓ Lighting. Consider upgrading, repairing or installing sensor- and timer-operated mounted floodlights, but only if the lights will display criminal activity to neighbours or passing traffic.

After completing the external survey, while it's fresh in your mind, review the problems and add any additional explanation you might need. 'Cat' may be all you wrote originally about the utility room window; you may need to add something to remind you to get everyone to lock it whenever you go out!

A word of warning: your notes would be a gift to any potential burglar if they were found, because they list all vulnerabilities in your home, so keep them safe.

CARRYING OUT AN INTERNAL SECURITY SURVEY

Now we start looking inside the house. Start at the front door and work your way through every room on the ground floor, then all other floors, but don't start until you have read this chapter.

Shared occupancy

In single-occupancy accommodation you can lock up when you leave; in shared-occupancy accommodation your control is limited. This makes the security risk in shared-occupancy accommodation 20 times higher than that in single-occupancy. The smaller the private area you control the greater the threat.

■ Single occupants have total control; they can lock the house and nobody should be there when they are out.

■ Shared occupants share access and security with others, hence they have less control and less security.

■ Students may share kitchen and bathroom, and only have a small room they can call their own, meaning that their bedroom door is their barrier on the world. Lock it, even if you are only going to the toilet; you don't know who is around, staying or visiting!

■ If you share a room with several people you can guarantee security only when you are in the room and awake. Alternatively, you can guarantee security of items only if you carry them with you.

Shared occupancy – countermeasures

✓ Be aware of the problems associated with shared occupancy.

✓ If you are forced to share insecure accommodation, consider the wisdom of buying portable valuables and keeping them in your room.

✓ Consider buying a solid lockable steel cabinet, which you can use to store your valuables while you are out of the room.

✓ Never leave money, credit cards etc. unattended and in view – and vulnerable.

✓ Consider leaving more valuable property with relatives. You can retrieve your video camera from Aunt Susan if you need it next week.

✓ Keep records of the make and serial number of each item of your property.

✓ Foster a security-conscious spirit among fellow residents in your area. Encourage them to agree to lock their street door, never let anyone in that they don't recognize and, most important, challenge strangers, particularly:
  • anyone who is not recognized by residents;
  • anyone who looks flustered or surprised;
  • anyone carrying or removing anything from neighbours' premises (without proof or corroboration, don't believe anyone who says they are taking the DVD player and television or laptop computer for repair).

Fire

While you are performing your survey, do a fire safety assessment as well. Your local fire and rescue staff can help with this, but you can make common-sense checks immediately.

Smoke detectors Smoke detectors save lives; if you don't have any, get some installed immediately!

Fire – countermeasures

✓ If you do have smoke detectors, check their positioning.

✓ Change the batteries regularly. I advise you to do this twice a year – once on your birthday and once six months later.

✓ Push the test button at least once each month.

Check for threats Check for fire threats in each room. The fire and rescue service can help with leaflets and visits to advise you. Paraffin heaters used to be a major risk; overloaded sockets, damaged electrical wires and forgotten cooking pans are still threats.

About one third of fire-related household deaths in the UK are attributed to smoking. Smokers are almost twice as likely as non-smokers to have a house fire.

Fire threats – countermeasures

✓ Any device should be plugged into a wall socket that has been installed by a qualified electrician.

✓ Trailing cables, extension leads and adapters are signs that a house needs to be rewired – don't wait too long. (If you are buying a house, ask when it was last rewired and if necessary reduce your offer by the price of rewiring.)

✓ It is recommended that UK domestic wiring should be professionally tested at least every ten years. When was yours last tested?

✓ Faulty electric systems kill; have remedial work done immediately by qualified tradesmen.

✓ No smoking in bedrooms (don't fall asleep while smoking).

✓ No smoking in the lounge (discarded cigarettes cause fires in furnishings).

✓ No smoking in the garage (danger of fuel or other flammable material igniting).

✓ Consider asking all smokers to step outside to smoke. It is better for your health, the safety of your home, preserving your furnishings and decorations.

✓ Standing rules. Consider establishing standing rules and procedures for the home. If every member of the family agrees and there is a standard list, everybody can easily comply. The following list includes non-fire-related rules.
  • Never leave electrical appliances switched on while they are unattended.
  • Never smoke cigarettes in the house.
  • The last person to leave the house must make sure all windows and doors are locked.
  • Smoke detectors must never be disconnected, or have their batteries removed to be used in portable CD players or games consoles or any other electrical appliance.
  • Smoke detector batteries will be replaced on the birth date of the head of the household and six months after that.
  • Pans will never be left unattended on the cooker.
  • Valuables and other property will never be left on show near windows or in unattended cars.
  • Cars will always be locked when left unattended.
  • Car keys will never be left in an unattended vehicle even for a minute.
  • Inform local relatives or close friends if you are going to be away from home for more than a day or so.

Practice escapes Escaping from your home in the dark, with alarms sounding and heat and smoke beginning to rise, is more traumatic than most people realize. It is easy to get disoriented even in your own home, so arrange practice evacuations, especially if you have children.

If adults only are involved, arrange a realistic practice evacuation. Take it in turns to blindfold one resident and assign an escort to keep them safe. Turn the blindfolded escapee around a few times then declare a fire in a given location, such as the hall or the kitchen and see if they can escape. Do this against the clock to make it realistic; in a real fire you wouldn't hang around!

Children's practice escapes With young children it is more difficult. You must maintain their trust in you and their feeling of safety within the home. Don't push too hard and don't scare them. Though you have serious intentions, make it fun; a competition and 'grown-up' game for younger children. Award them prizes for remembering what to do and doing it right.

Try to ease children into the practice, for example on a day when they say they have had a fire drill at school. They know then that fire drills have to be carried out sometimes. Ask them how they did the drill at school and tell them you want to see how clever they are and how quickly they can get out of their own house in a fire drill. Give them an easy start by sitting in the lounge, then tell them the competition has started and that they must get out and stand by the front gate or wherever you define as your meeting point. (*Nothing* is more frightening or disorienting than a building on fire. The only easy way of checking that everyone is out is to arrange a meeting point outside.)

When you are practising evacuation with your children, offer them plenty of praise and support to encourage them. Make sure that the children are rewarded with a trip to the cinema or their choice of day out – anything that reinforces the exercise as a pleasant experience and nothing to be worried about.

When the first exercises have been successfully completed increase the complexity. Get them to lie on their beds and then knock on the doors and tell them to leave. Over time, with plenty of praise, you can make the exercise more difficult and more realistic by doing it at night in the dark.

If children misunderstand or make a mistake, never tell them off or get angry, just point out where they could do better. Allow them to take a turn as the leader and, in consultation with Mum or Dad, choose where the 'fire' has been discovered and so define the safe escape route. Children must be able to get out of the house alone if you are not available.

Some key points to remember are:

- Evacuations prepare your child and family members for real evacuations elsewhere so that they are ready to escape when an alarm sounds at home, in the cinema, at the football stadium or sports hall.

- ALWAYS make sure that everyone knows when there is a practice evacuation. Then they know that any other alarm is *real* and they must act accordingly.

- Don't practise too often; the exercise will become stale and boring and will lose its impact.

- With any evacuation, somebody should know how many people are in the building. They should act as leader and attend the meeting point outside with a notebook or other means of ticking off names to check people are out of the building. They should also note other information they can give the fire officers, such as 'Top floor is clear; no sign of fire' or 'Everyone is out of the building; there is a chip pan fire in the kitchen.'

■ When the fire engines arrive, the leader should be able to brief firemen on what happened, giving them any information on possible hazards. For example, 'Everyone is out. I was welding my old motorbike and a fire has started. There are welding gas cylinders in the garage, and a motorbike with a full fuel tank.'

■ The leader should also make notes on how the evacuation went, looking for things that worked well and things that didn't work so well. Take another look at the meeting place; if it is subject to flooding in heavy rain, select a new meeting place that will be dry.

■ Practise the evacuation procedures too. For example:
  - Crouch down low. Smoke and heat rise so, in a fire, the air will be clearer lower down. Crawl along the floor towards the exit.
  - If necessary, and if it is possible to do so without delaying your exit from the building, consider covering your mouth and nose with a wet towel.
  - Try to protect young children. In a real fire they may become scared and hide under the bed instead of leaving. Don't assume they have left, look for them. (This is where practice drills pay dividends.)

- If necessary, cover all exposed skin with natural materials, such as wool blankets; avoid man-made fabrics.
- Always have slip-on footwear available in your bedroom. While evacuating you may be walking through red-hot cinders or broken glass.
- In a burning building, feel the door with the back of your hand. If it feels hot there may be an inferno on the other side. If the door feels OK, carefully touch the door handle with the back of your hand – don't just grab it. If the door is hot and the handle is even hotter, assume there is a fire on the other side of the door and find another exit.

Torches Keep a torch with working batteries beside your bed.

Windows The best and safest escape route is out through a door. If the stairs are blocked by fire, a window might be your only escape route. Though current regulations require double-glazing units to open fully to allow escape through upper-floor windows, older units may not meet those regulations. Check the upstairs windows, and replace them if you need to.

Doors Though security is our primary consideration, in an emergency you need to be able to leave the property quickly. Lock your doors but leave a key to hand so that you can find it quickly if you need to. Perhaps keep it on a hook near the door at night so that you always know where to find it. Release bolts and chains so that if you need to you can escape quickly.

Flood

Flooding is a hazard that more UK families are facing. While you are reviewing your home security, check with your local authority and water supply company. They can usually tell you if your house is susceptible to flooding. Include a flooding check on any home you are thinking of buying. You can get this information from www.environment-agency.gov.uk

Front door

The front door is important because it is usually the access point that faces the world and the one that is most used. As you enter, check the quality and strength of the door.

Keys hidden outside Keep a spare key with a local relative or trusted friend, but don't leave or hide one outside. No matter how clever you think you are with your hiding place, a burglar could find it. Don't give him a key.

Hidden key – countermeasures

✓ Don't hide keys outside.

✓ If you have to have emergency keys, give one to each of two relatives or very close friends who live nearby. Why two? One of them might be out when you need your emergency key!

✓ Make sure that you trust your key holders and anyone who lives with them. Mrs Biggin from number 42 may be a wonderful lady, but her daughter's drug addict boyfriend is not as trustworthy.

Softwood door Many doors are made of cheap softwoods. They have little real strength and one kick will usually break them open. Swing the door on its hinges, you will feel the weight of the door. Gently try to twist it; how much movement is there? A good solid door will *feel* good and solid.

Door panels Some door designs include a weakness that is well known to criminals. Door panels set into the door often have very little strength and may be just plywood. One kick and the panel flies out, leaving access to a burglar.

Hardwood door A hardwood door is much more secure. If you swing it back and forth you will be able to feel the weight.

UPVC (double-glazed) UPVC (plastic) double-glazed doors appear to be secure because of their multiple-point locking mechanisms, but many suffer from panel weakness and are vulnerable to a simple kick. Newer and more expensive doors have steel frames built into the carcass of the door which, combined with the multiple-locking-point mechanisms do make them very secure, but steel frames are rarely found in older doors.

Door frame The quality and fixing of the door frame are as important as the quality of the door. If the frame is weak and badly fitted it will give way and the strength of the door is then irrelevant. Weaknesses include the following.

- The frame is constructed of cheap wood or is rotten.

- The frame is secured with the wrong fittings or not enough fittings were used.

- The structure of the wall to which the frame is secured may be substandard.

- The frame may be the wrong size for the opening it has been used in.

Locks

No matter how strong the door is, it has one fundamental flaw and that is that doors are designed and built to swing open easily. They should also be able to be locked securely when required and that is achieved by fitting quality locks and bolts. The effectiveness of the security of any door depends just as much on the quality, number, fixing and placement of locks and bolts.

A night latch is convenient because it secures the door and the owner only needs to carry a small key to allow them to open and close the lock. The night latch usually screws to the surface of the door, so offers minimal protection against physical assault. As a single-point fastening, the night latch offers poor protection because one solid kick will break the door open.

A two-point locking scheme offers better protection, especially if the second locking point uses a 5-lever mortice deadlock (which fits inside the door) to British Standard BS3621.

Different locksmiths give different advice as to the type, location and fixing of door locks. Technically, the advice will differ depending on a number of factors:

■ the premises in question and what they hold – security for a dustbin store will be different from a bank's;

■ access to the door. Whether it would be possible for a ram raider to drive at the door, or whether it only has pedestrian access;

▦ the length of time the door will be exposed to a threat. If a night patrol checks the door every 15 minutes, the maximum exposure time of that door to a threat will be 15 minutes;

▦ the material used to make the door. Softwood doors are quite weak, UPVC with a steel core is very strong, but not as strong as a steel vault door;

▦ the skills and experience used to install the door. A good door badly installed offers reduced security;

▦ the design and presence of windows. A door fitted with louvres is weak. Similarly, glass in or beside a door reduces security. Why fit a strong door if any lout with a brick can break the window to get in?

French window/patio door

French windows are probably the most vulnerable door in any property. Usually located at the rear of the premises, they allow a criminal to work unobserved and uninterrupted. Designed to let in light and be easily opened wide to give access to the garden, they are often designed more for looks and access than for solid security. They can often easily be levered open with simple tools, unless the owner has taken steps to secure them.

Door security – countermeasures

✓ Buy the best door you can afford and can justify for the use you have in mind.

✓ Have the door installed by a skilled tradesman.

✓ Ensure that the frame is of equal quality and that it is firmly and correctly secured to the surrounding masonry.

✓ Use the best hinges suitable for the application.

✓ Install hinge bolts, fitted into the hinge edge of the door. They reinforce and strengthen the door on the hinge side.

✓ Use at least a two-point fastening scheme. Your locksmith will advise you where to fit the locks, but generally it is advised that one lock is fitted approximately two fifths of the way down from the top of the door and another just under half way up from the bottom. At least one lock should be a properly installed mortice lock.

✓ Always lock the lock when you go out.

✓ For safety reasons DON'T leave the mortice lock locked when you are in the house, particularly at night, in case you need to get out of the house in a hurry. Use the night latch and leave the key in it for easy escape!

✓ Carefully check any French windows and patio doors. If in any doubt get them checked by an expert.

Other door furniture

Depending on their use, doors may need other fixtures and fittings, which are collectively known as 'door furniture'. For example:

Letterbox Cutting a hole weakens the structure of the door. Criminals fish through a letterbox to remove car keys and valuables left within reach. A letterbox should be fitted by a tradesman in a door designed to have a letterbox. Follow manufacturers recommendations. The letterbox should:

▪ be large enough to accommodate letter and postal deliveries;

▪ be conveniently situated – the postman will not be happy with a letter box at the bottom of the door.

Window bars Where windows are fitted beside doors, fitting window bars or grilles provides an added deterrent and an extra measure of security, but may be unsightly.

Hinge bolts are fitted to and reinforce the hinge side of the door. They are fitted at intervals along the hinge edge of the door. I usually advise fitting three.

Internal door furniture

Other door furniture can be used inside the door, some of which is primarily used to increase security and some have secondary security benefits. For example:

Mail basket A metal basket inside the letterbox catches incoming post, but it also stops burglars from fishing through to hook car and door keys off hall tables. Never keep keys in the hall or near the front or other doors.

Letterbox covers Inside a letterbox, designed to stop draughts and can prevent rodents and insects from entering through a letterbox. If spring-loaded, they will hinder visibility and access to criminals.

Draught excluders A draft excluder is a warning sign to me; it tells me that the door doesn't fit properly and is therefore a security risk. If you see a draft excluder, check the door thoroughly.

Weather strip A weather strip may also indicate that the door does not fit properly so take a closer look.

Door viewer/spy hole Fitted to a solid door they allow you to see who is outside without opening the door. Once fitted, ask somebody to hide to the right or left of the door, then check to see if you can see them using the door viewer. This will help you to identify any blind spots where a potential attacker could hide. Identify and remove blind spots by blocking them with trellis. Force visitors to stand where you can see them.

Door chains Door chains allow a door to be opened a little, without giving access to intruders. They have the same limitations. They have to be fitted properly, and they only work if they are used. If you have one – use it. (Don't leave the door chain on at night though, make escape easy if you need to leave.)

Notices and signs Notices and signs can be a deterrent, increasing security and preventing nuisance. Signs such as 'We do not buy from doorstep salesmen', 'No free newspapers or circulars', 'Door alarmed', 'Patrolled by ABC Security' or 'CCTV in use' can deter unwanted callers.

Notes Avoid leaving notes on the door. A note saying 'Gone out – all deliveries to number 42' is a Christmas present to a criminal, who now knows the house is empty. Worse still, 'On holiday – no milk until Saturday 27th' gives the burglar up to two weeks to check over your house.

Top and bottom locks Additional security can be obtained by fitting bolts at the top and bottom of a door. They make it a lot harder to break down a door, but I question their value if the door is already fitted with hinge bolts and a two-point locking system. Additional bolts can only be used when you are inside, and you don't want to use them at night while you are in bed, because they might block or delay your escape in an emergency.

Windows Windows beside doors can make the hall lighter, but glass is too easy to break so I advise against ordering doors with glass panels. Why install a really solid and expensive security door, when the window next to it can be removed with half a brick.

Windows – countermeasures

✓   Avoid glass in doors and beside doors.

✓   If glass is present, consider replacing the door and possibly replacing the side windows with more secure options.

✓   If you have windows in or beside a door, consider fitting metal grills to make them more secure. (Remember that a landlord may have objections to any of this work and with listed buildings it may be a problem.)

Entrance hall

Now you should start reviewing the security of the rooms inside your property. Move from room to room, paying particular attention to the access points, especially those that connect to the world outside. They are the points that could give access to criminals if they are insecure.

The first room is the entrance hall, and that is unique because you should already have considered the front door and will consider any alarm system separately. Look at the rest of the hall with security in mind.

Keys There should be no keys visible or accessible from the front door.

Lighting There should be a switch to operate bright external porch lights, allowing you to see clearly who is at the door. (If you switch on the porch light and it doesn't work, maybe the bulb has blown or maybe a criminal has removed the bulb – keep that door chain on!)

Dressing the hall Elderly people may benefit from 'stage dressing' their hall. If a visitor to the front door sees a headscarf, a coat and shoes in the style that an older woman would wear, he can guess that perhaps an elderly woman lives there alone. If she dresses her hall with the help of younger relatives or items from a charity shop she can change what the visitor sees. A strong, used dog lead hanging beside the coat indicates a large dog living in the house. Football boots, a man's jacket and baseball cap indicate to a caller with less than good intentions, that there may be a younger man around somewhere or due back soon. Remember, anything that deters a criminal is worthwhile.

Alarm system

Below are questions you should be asking about alarms.

■ Is there an alarm system? Is it working? How often has it been triggered, and what triggered it? (If it is badly installed or adjusted it may be useless.)

■ What points of access are covered by the alarm and by what method (contact breaker, pressure pads, movement sensors, heat sensors, light beams, break-glass detectors etc.). Are all access points covered (that new patio door may have been put in since the alarm was installed so it isn't alarmed)?

■ Is the burglar alarm system monitored by the company who supplied it, or does it rely on neighbours calling the police?

■ Are there any panic buttons? If so, where are they located?

■ How often is the alarm used – that is, switched on rather than left switched off? (Some people rarely use them.)

■ Who has the key or code needed to turn the alarm off or on? Previous owners or tenants had the code, plus any cleaners, builders and other workers who may have been given it. Children can be careless, allowing people to see or know the code. If you are in any doubt, change the code.

■ Does the system have a record of activating for no apparent reason?

Alarm – countermeasures

✓ A system that is never used is not worth having.

✓ A system that goes off too often will be ignored by everyone.

✓ A system that does not cover all access points is not worth having.

✓ If the alarm sounds, there is a reason. Use extreme caution when checking the premises. If there are any signs of criminal activity, such as broken glass or open doors, call the police.

✓   If the alarm sounds and you disturb an intruder, make as much noise as you can to scare them away. They will want to escape and you shouldn't try any heroics. Better that they get away than you are injured or killed trying to catch them.

✓   A dummy alarm box will put off opportunists, but it will not fool a career criminal.

✓   Beware of the return visit. Criminals sometimes deliberately trigger an alarm then hide. They may do it several times, waiting for the owner to decide it is a fault and turn the alarm off until the engineer can check it next day. That is when criminals come out of hiding and take what they want, undisturbed.

Ground-floor rooms

You should now work methodically to check all ground-floor rooms in order. In each room pay particular attention to doors, windows and skylights in external walls and ceilings because that is where intruders might find access.

Ground-floor windows

Check that all ground-floor windows can be fully closed and locked. Are the keys to window locks in the locks or have they been removed and held in a safe place? Check the fit of the window; is it loose, does it rattle? Is there any sign of rot in a wooden frame? Check the window and frame for stability; is it loose or well fitted? Make a note of any problems.

At night leave bedroom windows unlocked. If there is a fire you may want to escape using the windows.

Ground-floor doors

Ground-floor doors and windows are most vulnerable to attack. Criminals prefer to use doors because it is easier for them to get in and out of your house, especially when they are carrying your television and laptop computer. Check the fit, quality, locks and stability of all ground-floor doors, then note any problems.

Basement

Check security in any basement or cellar you may have. Pay particular attention to traditional access points like doors and windows, but don't forget things like coal delivery chutes. Check the locks and quality of the door that leads from the house down into the basement. Note any problems.

Upper-floor doors

Work your way up to and around each upper floor. Check all windows and doors, paying particular attention to any that open on to a flat roof, a balcony or anywhere an intruder may have easy access.

Beware of any balcony or flat roof that gives access to adjoining properties; they give easy access to your home too. These upper-floor doors should be made as secure as the front door to any property, while still allowing for easy escape in a fire.

On any balcony or flat roof, it is worth checking for access routes and hand and foot holds from above, below and to the side. Do not climb or lean out yourself, note any problems.

Loft/loft conversion

If you have an attic or loft you should check it for security, but be careful if you do. Most lofts don't have floorboards so there is a danger that you could fall through into one of the rooms below.

I once performed a security survey on a terrace home to find that the dividing walls between lofts were incomplete. It was possible to climb through the roof spaces, giving easy access to every house in the terrace!

While you are checking the loft, check the quality and security of the loft hatch and any windows in the gable end walls or the roof. Take time to check for broken tiles, leaking pipes or wasp's nests, the state of the lagging etc. Note any problems and get an expert to check them.

KEEPING TRACK OF YOUR HOUSE KEYS

Before you go any further, sit down and make a note of how many sets of keys there are to your house and who holds them. When you have finished your list, read on.

How many sets of keys have you listed – three, maybe four? You think you know how many sets of keys are in circulation, but how many *could* be in circulation?

Who has a key to your house?

When you buy a house, one or two sets of keys are passed to you by the former owner, but most families have more than two sets of keys.

Previous owners may have kept keys for sentimental reasons – 'our first house' – or given a forgotten set of keys to a relative or to the lady who used to clean for them. Maybe their plumber has a forgotten set from the time he put in a new boiler five years ago. The man at number 73 has a garage key from when he serviced their car. Young Jason lost his keys at school three times so they are still missing. Add six or seven estate agents over the years, and it all begins to add up.

Compare how many sets of keys you thought existed with the number of sets that may exist. Improving home security is pointless if half the population of the county may have keys to your home. If you don't control keys, you don't control your security. Seriously consider changing the locks. Compared to the price of the house and the contents you might lose, that is a cheap and sensible option.

How careful are you with your keys?

Control over the number of sets of keys that are in circulation is important to maintaining security, but how careful are you with your keys?

On a hook in the kitchen or sitting in the hall they may not be safe. We know that burglars fish keys out through letterboxes. Window cleaners have been known to snatch keys, have copies cut and then return the originals when they come in to rinse a sponge. They then have a duplicate key and a list of valuables to sell off to a burglar. All your keys should be kept out of sight and out of reach of the door and any visitors who are passing through.

Keys – countermeasures

✓ Locks give you security, keys give you access, so be strict in managing and controlling your keys.

✓ Never leave your keys unattended. Don't leave them in your car ignition while you open the garage door, or in an unattended bag while you nip to the toilet. (Handbags and cases often also hold something that shows your address, so the bag thief gets your keys *and* your address.)

✓ Never leave any keys inside windows, on your desk at work, in your car – in fact, anywhere that they may be taken or copied.

✓ Don't put your address or car number on a key tag. Don't make it easy for criminals to make a visit and help themselves to your valuables.

✓ Label your keys with your mobile phone number so that if you lose them the finder can call you. DON'T give your address – they may be honest, they may not be. Arrange to meet at a mutually convenient public place, such as the library or a supermarket, take possession of your keys, but consider changing all the locks anyway.

✓ Know how many keys you have cut for any given lock and record who has each key.

✓ Before you issue anyone with a key, ask yourself if they really need their own key. If it's for their convenience don't weaken your security and don't issue a key; they can wait to be let in by somebody else. Minimize the number of people who have keys and so have independent access to your home.

✓ When people such as cleaners or workmen move on keep control of their keys. Make sure you get them back and if you are in any doubt of their honesty change the locks.

✓ How many keys do you carry? Most people carry a few that they can't identify. Spring-clean your key ring today. Do you really need all the keys you carry? Old keys, keepsakes and unknown keys can all be removed from your key ring. The shed key can go in a drawer in the kitchen. Put unknown keys in a sealed envelope and write 'unknown keys' with a date on the envelope and store them in the back of the garage – just in case.

✓ Never allow strangers unattended access to your keys.

✓ Get all key holders to secure their keys and agree to keep them safe. If they won't agree, they don't get a key!

✓ Avoid using key racks which are helpfully labelled 'BMW', 'Garage', 'Speedboat', etc.

✓ What if you find that a key doesn't fit any longer? It's not unknown for criminals simply to switch keys. This takes a second and the loss may not be noticed for weeks. All you know is that you still have three keys on your key ring; you won't notice the switch if you never use the back door key. During that time the thief has free access to your home through the back door. If you don't need it, don't carry it; and if it suddenly doesn't fit, change the locks.

✓ If you lose a key, or take over a property, you should change the locks to regain control and maintain security.

✓ When you are managing your keys, keep the number of keys to a minimum.

✓ If your circumstances change, review your register of key holders. Make any necessary changes and always consider changing the locks if you need to.

✓ For extra security you can buy a security lock, which means that keys can only be cut at specialist security stores, not at any old shoe repair shop or market stall.

✓ If you fit security locks make sure that the locks are registered to you and not to the locksmith who fits them. If you need new keys only the person the lock is registered to can order keys and if that is the locksmith they can make a new key very expensive.

✓ Consider issuing one key, not a set of keys. If you have children, only issue them with a single key, either to the front or the back door (whichever lock is easiest and cheapest to replace). If that key is lost you will only have to replace one lock; if they lost a set of keys you would have to replace all locks.

✓ Make sure no keys are accessible through open windows, letterboxes etc. – fit a mail basket internal flap and a brush draught excluder as well to prevent 'fishing'.

✓ If you have a cleaner, lodger or any other non-family member of the household, replace all locks to which they had a key when the relationship is terminated.

✓ Don't leave house keys in your car. If the car is broken into, the criminal has your house keys, and probably your full address from documents in the car.

✓ When your car is serviced or repaired take the car key off your key ring and leave that with the garage. Don't give them a chance to copy your house keys.

✓ If your keys were in your car, coat, briefcase or anything else that has been stolen, change the locks.

✓ Never, ever leave house keys with a builder or other workmen.

✓ Never leave keys with estate agents or anyone else. When you hand a key to an organization rather than a person, you have totally and irrevocably breached your security.

RECORDING THE DETAILS OF YOUR HOUSE
CONTENTS

As part of your security survey, perform a survey of the valuable contents. Walk through all your rooms again, making a note of valuable contents, particularly things that a thief might take. Check in drawers, cupboards, wardrobes, trunks etc., to record jewellery, the digital camera in your sock drawer and any other valuable item.

Take photographs of items, record descriptions and serial numbers, and mark the items with your post code and house number using a UV pen. One insurance company reported that only 14% of people claiming for stolen property knew the make, model and serial number of the item(s) stolen. If you can't identify it, you are very unlikely to get it back.

For a flat screen television you might record:

■   item description (e.g. flat-screen 42-inch television);

■   make (e.g. Panasonic);

■   item model (e.g. Model PS/345-2v);

■   serial number (e.g. P87-FS8650-7642-22);

■   unique marks (1 inch 'x'-shaped scratch above 'on/off' switch)

■   other information (for example, if you were recording jewellery, a valuation and date given);

■   whether or not a photograph has been taken;

■   whether the item is marked with a postcode and, if so, where it is marked.

Your 'valuable contents survey' will allow you to keep a record of your valuables, including a description, make, model, serial number, identification marks and reference to any picture or video footage you may have. See the example below.

Description	Make	Model	Serial Number	Unique Marks	Other Information	Photograph
Lounge television	Panasonic	PS/345-2v	P87-FS8650-7642-22	X-shaped scratch above 'on/off' switch	38-inch flat screen	
Grandmother's clock — on dining room mantel	Wilson & Wilson	N/A	546-4	Chip on case to left of winding hole	Valued at £2,300 Aug 1991 by Acres Antiques	Property album 3 pictures 17 to 19 plus videotape 3 at 1hr 20 minutes through the tape
Digital camera, Dad's room	Minolta	MD-546-3	MD-29875611	Contains chip with pictures of our dog	Taken with blue canvas camera bag	N/A

Photographs

Photographs make finding lost or stolen property a lot easier, even for something as simple as a bicycle. The value of a picture will increase where a size scale such as a (12 inch) 30-cm ruler is in shot.

Take photographs from the front, rear and sides of anything that is hard to describe (jewellery, antiques, ceramics, artwork etc.). Keep the pictures with your 'valuables list', and keep the negatives or digital image for future use.

Videotape

Videotape film can help to show valuables. A tour of your house featuring key items is a huge bonus when describing the contents of the home. The tape can also help to identify/remember what is missing after a raid and help with insurance valuations after a fire or other disaster.

Do you tell the criminals what you have

You don't think you do, but you might! We are still considering the house, more specifically what you throw out.

Flat-screen televisions and laptops etc. all come in boxes which clearly show their contents. We unpack them then put the box out for the dustman/recycling, telling any passing criminal that we have just unpacked a brand new computer, DVD player or whatever. Don't advertise it; either take the box to a recycling centre yourself or, if you have to put it out for collection, cut the box and put the markings on the inside so that nobody can see what was in it.

Information theft/identity theft

A sift through the rubbish bin of many houses will produce an alarming amount of information, such as:

- pay statements/pay slips;

- income tax documents;

- cash withdrawal receipts;

- utility bills;

- credit card statements and receipts, showing numbers and expiry dates.

The UK suffers from more identity theft than Germany, Ireland, Netherlands and Belgium combined. It accounts for £1.2 billion a year. 5 million people have now been victims of identity theft and recorded identity theft is up significantly on last year.

Identity theft is a crime that is growing out of control. Check before throwing anything out, and shred anything that holds personal details of any kind.

Information theft/identity theft – countermeasures

✓   Destroy any documents that hold personal information. You can throw away advertisements or instructions on how to pay etc., but first extract anything with personal information on and destroy it.

Scissors Snip papers into tiny shreds with your scissors.

Fire If you have space and time, you can have a monthly bonfire of personal information. Be safe, make sure that papers don't blow away before they have burned, or stay half burned after the fire goes out.

Office shredder Some employers don't object to staff bringing in and shredding the occasional document. Check first, and don't abuse this privilege.

Home shredder A home cross-cut shredder costing about £40 is adequate. CAUTION – if it is abused a shredder can be dangerous and shredded paper is a fire hazard.

Security waste-disposal companies Commercial companies offer secure shredding services. They are not cheap, and are usually only worth considering for domestic use if you are sorting out papers before moving or when a relative has died etc.

✓   Don't give personal information over the telephone (including mobiles) unless you are absolutely sure of the identity of the person calling.

✓ If you really need to give personal details, only do it if *you* telephone *them* and you can confirm their number, for example from your bank statement, or from a telephone directory.

✓ NEVER call people back on phone numbers they give you to pass personal information – you could be phoning a criminal.

✓ The Internet is just another 'telephone call'. Criminals try to collect personal information via official-looking emails, for example fraudoffice@mybank.com but they are quite easy to create. Generally, the Internet and emails are not secure.

✓ Criminals easily create an official-looking website called WWW.SECURITYyourbank.COM. They ask you to prove your identity with your account number, credit card number, security code etc. Then they are spending your money abroad before you realize it is a dummy site. NEVER give personal, financial, medical or any other details over the Internet in any survey, quiz, competition or other transaction.

✓ Never trust a postal mail shot. It may look official, it may explain that everybody is switching cards for security reasons. They ask you to fill in your account number, expiry dates, security code details, confirm your mother's maiden name etc., and return it in the conveniently post paid envelope to Mr C. Riminal, Central Processing Centre, PO Box 1554, Crookstown. There goes some more of your money!

✓ Think before you fill in any form. Many organizations issue forms, for example, for extended warranty, a quote for a new kitchen, etc., and demand unnecessary information such as

'Do you own your own home?', 'Do you have a mortgage – if so, how much?' They are just collecting information on you. Only fill in relevant information. If they demand that information for no reason take your business elsewhere.

Then the criminals come back!

Criminals know that you will claim off your insurance and replace anything that has been stolen, replacing the missing items as soon as you can. It is quite common for criminals to wait to give you time to replace everything, then they come back (when they see all of those TV and laptop boxes outside, waiting to be collected) taking all the new possessions that you have only just unwrapped.

REPORTING AND FINDING LOST PROPERTY

Many people assume that once stolen they will never see their property again. ALWAYS report losses and theft to the police.

Police record items reported stolen or lost. They then check the details of suspect property against their records. If your stolen digital camera, Rolex watch, or other valuables come to light and are recorded on the database, you will get them back. If the details are not on there, the police do not know that they are lost or stolen so they are handed back to Billy Burglar.

Apart from the police databases there are a few online databases that you can search, for example www.virtualbumblebee.co.uk.

Consider recording your mobile phone and other electronic equipment on www.immobilise.com so that it can be traced back to you.

ISSUES THAT ARE UNIQUE TO YOU

Everybody is unique, so your survey should include additional issues that are unique to you and your lifestyle. You may own a stable and horses in a field over the road, or you may own a vintage car that you keep in a commercial store. Your security audit will be compromised if you ignore any of these unique issues relating to your house and lifestyle. Take some time to make sure that you have identified everything.

Be as thorough and conscientious as possible when completing your security review, and keep an open mind as to other issues that you should address.

Medical problems

Medical conditions could affect your life, your mobility or even the use of your house. For instance, an elderly disabled widow may stop using the upper floors of her house because she can no longer manage the stairs. The way people live and use their homes has a significant impact on their security requirements. That elderly woman may not realize she has been burgled for weeks. During your review take all circumstances into consideration.

Building work

If you employ builders or decorators, you will have a range of new security problems.

■ They need reasonable access to your home.

■ They may store valuable materials or tools around the property, which could attract criminal interest.

■ If they erect any scaffold or ladders, they will significantly reduce the security of your house.

Building work – countermeasures

✓ Insist that the workmen provide you with:
  • references as to the quality of their work;
  • references as to their ability to finish work within stated time, cost and quality targets;
  • assurances as to the honesty and integrity of their employees;
  • proof of insurance that covers you, your family and property for any injury, loss or damage caused by their own or their employees' and agents' oversight, actions, negligence, accidental or criminal acts.

✓ Before accepting bids and quotes, check all references supplied.

✓ Before the workmen arrive remove valuables from areas to which they have access.

✓ Never leave builders or other workers alone in your home, and certainly do not give them any keys to the premises.

✓ Arrange for the work to be done when an adult member of the family can be there to supervise them.

✓ Pay a deposit, but never pay the full cost of a job until it has been finished *to your satisfaction.*

✓ Never employ workmen who come and knock on your door. Without a genuine address you cannot check on them or contact them if there is a problem.

House insurance

The first point to remember is that the insurance industry exists to make a profit. Broadly speaking, there are two different types of household cover, building insurance and contents insurance.

Building insurance You can insure the structure of the building. If the house burns down, with appropriate cover the insurance company will pay for it to be rebuilt in the same style but complying with modern building regulations. *Warning*: check the cover supplied by your insurer. An insurer might specify conditions under which they will not cover your property against damage. Potential problems include:

■ flood – insurers may exclude flooding from your insurance cover;

■ subsidence – some areas are prone to subsidence, and in those areas the insurance company may exclude or limit cover for subsidence;

■ fire – more often seen abroad, in areas where brush fires are a problem, insurers could refuse cover unless bushes are cut down, sprinklers and hose outlets are installed etc.

Building insurance – countermeasures

✓ Before buying a property check with the current owner, estate agent, local authority and insurance companies to find out if there are any insurance restrictions on the property in question.

✓ Flooding problems:

- Don't buy a house that is at risk of flooding.
- Check the environment agency flood plain maps online at www.environment-agency.gov.uk.
- Where flooding is possible, minimize your risk. Avoid installing expensive equipment on the ground floor. Don't leave your property unattended when there is risk of flooding.
- Always call the flood lines to get an update on current flooding risks.
- When floods are possible:
  - ❖ Move vulnerable babies, people, pets and valuables to safety.
  - ❖ Move cars to safety on higher ground.
  - ❖ Unplug electrical equipment and take it upstairs (television, video recorder, sounds systems, fridge/ freezer, washing machine etc.).
  - ❖ Take personal possessions and documents upstairs.
  - ❖ Keep an eye on your neighbours. If they don't seem to be doing anything, especially if they are elderly or infirm, check that they are there and know there is a flood risk.
  - ❖ Dig out your insurance certificate and contact numbers, leave them available safe upstairs for easy use later.

- ❖ Be prepared to wait for the all-clear. Make sure you have food and bottled water. There may be no power so a gas heater and camping cooker may be useful.
- ❖ Beware of the fire risk: candles and camping stoves are dangerous. Have fire extinguishers handy.
- ❖ Make sure that you have enough prescription medication if you need it.
- ❖ To prevent back flow during a flood, stuff a sandbag into all downstairs toilets and place a weight over manhole covers. Put bath, sink and washbasin plugs in and weigh them down too. (Back flow is where flooding pushes sewage up through toilets, baths and sinks.)
- ❖ If possible, turn off the electricity and gas at the mains – and after a flood, don't turn it on again until it has been checked and approved by a qualified tradesman.

✓ If there is a restriction on the insurance cover of a property, seriously consider if you want to take the risk of buying an 'uninsurable' property.

✓ If you already own a property with insurance restrictions, find out why they were imposed and take steps to reduce the risks to the property where you can. For example, if subsidence is a problem, don't extract water from the surrounding land; in other words, don't use borehole pumps, and beware of planting large plants that draw moisture from the soil near the house.

✓ If your neighbours redesign their garden, radically changing levels and drainage, this will affect you. Discuss the problem with them and try to resolve it.

Contents insurance You can insure the contents of your house, such as carpets, curtains, clothes, television, washing machine, in fact all of the contents. If the house burns down a 'contents' policy will pay for replacements for everything that was lost.

Warning: that was a very oversimplified explanation of home insurance. Insurance varies so much that you must carefully review what insurance you require and need. Make sure your insurance cover is appropriate. Common insurance problems include:

■ Inadequate cover – many people find that the insured sum will not cover the cost of replacement of all of their possessions. Check the level of your cover.

■ Not new for old – without new for old cover, you only receive what the insurance company decides was the current value of the damaged item. If your television cost £900 when new five years ago, the insurance company may say it was only worth £200 when it was lost and that is all they will pay.

■ Single-item limit – some policies specify a limit to the value of single items covered under the policy. If the limit is, say, £750, that is the maximum they will pay for any item that was lost. You only get £750 for your brand new £1,100 television, and you only get £750 for your new £1,300 computer system. If your policy specifies a limit, you may lose out if you make a claim.

■ Valuable items not listed – even with a single-item limit, for an extra fee some policies offer extra cover on named items. Therefore you may be able to cover your 50-inch, £3,000 plasma television as a listed item. With very valuable items the insurance company will almost certainly impose minimum security requirements; if they are not met, the items are not covered.

■ Exemptions – some policies impose exemptions. For example, your flat-screen plasma television will be insured only when it is in your home. Take it to work at your own risk.

■ Negligence – insurers can refuse to meet a claim where they consider you were negligent. If you went to work and left the lights on and the front door open, you may not be able to claim if you come home nine hours later and find that your property has been stolen.

Contents insurance – countermeasures

✓ Check the value of the contents of your home to confirm that your insurance cover is adequate to replace everything. Move from room to room, making a note of the value of items in that room. Using broad categories is a good way of getting a ball park figure without itemizing everything in each room. Note a value of the items in the following categories in each room.

Furnishings – chairs, cushions, cupboard, table, sofa, curtains, carpets, rugs, etc.

Electrical – washing machine, TV, DVD player, computer, vacuum cleaner, microwave oven, etc.

Clothing – outerwear, underwear, hats, boots and shoes, formal wear, leisure wear, etc.

Possessions – watches, make-up, books, briefcase, handbag, etc.

Valuables – jewellery, stamp collection, antique clock, medals, etc.

✓ Draw up a list of everything in each room, not forgetting those things that are out of sight in the loft, the cellar, and in your cupboards and drawers. Don't list every shirt or pair of high heels, just add a category, for example shirts × 20, or heels × 12.

After a few days, walk through and check again. You may remember a few more valuables, like the digital camera you loaned to a cousin. When the list is complete assign a *replacement value* (how much it will cost to replace that item today) to everything on the list. Then it is easy to add up a total replacement value for all your possessions in the house.

When finished compare your calculated replacement value with the level of cover specified on your policy. If you are concerned make a more detailed valuation, or ask the insurance company to increase the level of your cover – try to arrange new for old cover.

✓ Check your pricing list against any single-item price limit. If there is a problem, resolve it with the insurance company, and get any changes in writing.

✓ If you have any particularly valuable items, make sure that your insurance policy actually covers them.

✓ Check your policy for any exemptions. Keep limits and exemptions in mind when you are arranging replacement cover.

✓   Make your best effort to protect your property; insurers may refuse to pay out on claims where they consider you have been negligent.

House manual

By law, you now have to provide a Home Information Pack if you want to sell your house, but for many years I have promoted the use of a 'House Manual'.

The House Manual is a collection of important information about your house that is as useful to you as it will be to anyone who buys your home.

Your house manual should be held in a four-ring binder so that if sections change they can easily be replaced, or if a section is needed in an emergency, it can be taken out and used, then put back.

Emergency pages should be laminated, to keep them readable even if you do need to take them into the kitchen when the washing machine is flooding the ground floor of the house.

I suggest it should contain the following sections, plus any information appropriate to you and your lifestyle.

Emergency information This should be held in alphabetic order, one entry to a page, and written in large print (making it easier to read at three in the morning when a leak has fused all the lights).

It should be laminated for durability, updated as soon as there is any change, and include photographs or diagrams where they will help, such as locations of water stopcocks, mains power isolation switches and fuses.

Contact information Containing contact information, in alphabetic order, using multiple entries. (Multiple entry means you list an entry under all relevant headings to help you find the information you want. Under 'S' you may insert Splatter & Son, decorators; under 'D' record the entry as Decorators – Splatter & Son, etc., and maybe an entry under 'P' for Painters.)

Any information you collect can be held in the manual, such as details of recommended builders, garden services, car repair services, plumber, etc.

Significant dates This section is more like a diary for the house. In it you will record any significant events relating to the house. For example:

Date	Event	Contact	Comment
3/2/2010	Whole house rewired	Live 'N' Kicking electricians, contact Bob Jones 01234 345 678	1-year guarantee expires 4/2/2011
11/12/2009	Double glazing installed	Take A Butchers – double-glazing company 01765 345 265	5-year guarantee expires 10/12/2012
11/4/2010	Central heating back boiler and gas fire replaced	The Boring Gas Fire Company 01567 876 356	3-year guarantee expires 10/4/2013

Unique selling point

The House Manual contains information that is invaluable to a new owner and will be a unique selling point for your house. It shows the prospective buyer that you have taken care of the house and the records relating to it, so you have almost certainly been as efficient in ensuring that all work undertaken has been of an acceptable quality and standard.

As well as showing when your guarantees run out, and who to call if there is a fault, the manual also contains details of honest and trustworthy tradesmen in the area, which is very rare and valuable information to most people.

3

Securing Your Home While You Are Away

Most people take a holiday away from home each year. While you are away, your house is unattended and vulnerable.

PLANNING AHEAD FOR SECURITY

In the excitement of planning your holiday remember that you should also be making your holiday arrangements with the security of your house in mind.

Deliveries

Don't draw attention to an unoccupied house by making it necessary for delivery drivers to leave notes, or worse still deliveries on your doorstep.

Deliveries – countermeasures

✓ Avoid ordering anything that may be delivered while you are away.

✓ If an order may come while you are away, ask for it to be delivered direct to a relative or trusted neighbour.

✓ Just in case, ask a friend or neighbour to visit the house to check for deliveries.

Notes to tradesmen

Never leave notes on your door, such as 'Milkman, we are on holiday. No milk until 18 August', or perhaps, 'On holiday until 18 August. All deliveries to number 7, please.' Even a note saying 'Gone to shops, back in five minutes' may be enough to tempt a burglar.

Notes to tradesmen – countermeasures

✓ Arrange matters so that notes aren't necessary. Don't leave deliveries outstanding and consider cancelling regular deliveries while you are away.

✓ Tell the milkman personally that you don't want any milk until 18 August. Never leave a note outside advertising your absence.

✓ If you are in any doubt about your milkman's trustworthiness don't cancel the milk. It will cost you a few pounds, but things will look normal to any passing burglar, and a trusted neighbour or relative can visit daily to take in the milk.

✓ Arrange for a trusted relative or neighbour to collect mail etc. to clear the letterbox.

Junk mail and circulars

Your letterbox and front step are important to maintaining your security. Unwanted deliveries like free newspapers, circulars and pizza advertisements all get pushed into your letterbox or get dumped on the doorstep. This rubbish advertises to anyone passing that nobody is at home to clear it away.

Junk mail and circulars – countermeasures

✓   Arrange for a relative or friend to visit and clear your mail and check that there is no unwanted milk each day while you are away. Free newspapers can quickly block the letterbox or pile up on the doorstep.

✓   I saw a house with a dedicated delivery slot for circulars and free newspapers. Actually it was a delivery slot next to the front door, inside of which was a removable box. Every few days the owner removes the box, keeps anything interesting and throws the rest straight into the recycling bin.

✓   To stop most junk mail, try contacting the Mail Preference Service. Please see www.mpsonline.org.uk for details to register your desire to be excluded from junk mail postings. It doesn't stop all junk mail but it considerably reduces the amount. You need a valid email address to complete the online process, and it can take up to four months to have full effect. (See www.fpsonline.org.uk to register to be excluded from junk fax advertising, and www.tpsonline.org.uk to register to be excluded from unsolicited telephone advertising.)

✓   The Telephone Preference Service deals with telephone marketing. They can be contacted on 0845 0700707 or by emailing tps@dma.org.uk. All you have to do is register your phone numbers and you should be excluded from most UK-based telephone marketing.

Central heating

Winter cold snaps can damage your house while you are away.

Central heating – countermeasures

✓ Ensure that your central heating has been properly serviced, and maintained. If this is the case you can be pretty sure that it will not develop a fault and cause any problem. Your visiting friend or relative can do a quick walk through each day to check this.

✓ In winter, consider leaving your central heating on at a low level to prevent the pipes from freezing. This will also keep the house dry and warm for your return.

Lights on timers

When you are away, try to make your house look as occupied and lived in as possible. Anything you can do to make it look as if somebody is at home will be an extra deterrent to passing criminals.

Timers that plug into electrical sockets, allowing you to operate lights etc. at pre-set times are readily available. You can easily make lights go on and go off at times that match your normal pattern of activity.

The better electrical timers have a battery backup function so that they will keep working at the pre-set times even if there has been a power cut at some stage.

Lights on timers – countermeasures

✓ Only buy safe and approved electrical timers, that will not cause a fire while they are left unattended.

✓ Use timers sparingly; don't make your house look like seaside illuminations with all sorts of things switching on and off at different times.

✓ Make sure that you have some table or standard lamps that can be operated by the timers.

✓ Timer lights look better if you arrange for a relative or trusted neighbour to visit the house to draw curtains in the evening and open them in the morning.

✓ Use timers strategically, and plan their use. Use them to follow your lifestyle pattern. If you get up at six each morning, have a bedroom light that comes on at six. If you sit in the lounge from five until ten in the evenings, then go to bed, use timers to operate lights to indicate that pattern of movement.

Radio talk stations

Lights give the illusion of occupancy, and leaving a radio on should help with that illusion. Put the radio on a timer switch and tune it to a talk station. Music stations are OK, but if intruders outside hear 'people' talking, they will look for an easier and safer target down the road.

Radio talk station – countermeasures

✓ Buy or keep a timer switch to operate the radio.

✓ Tune the radio to a station that you know will be all talk such as a news and current affairs discussion channel.

✓ Tune the radio accurately, a crackling badly tuned hissing station will not fool anyone.

✓ Set the volume to a subdued conversational level. If it is set too loud people will realize it is the radio.

The garden

An uncut and overgrown lawn, or wilting hanging baskets and weeds invading your usually immaculate flowerbeds all tell the criminal that you are not at home. If you always trim the hedge on Sunday, then suddenly leave it for two weeks in August, criminals will draw their own conclusions.

Garden-based evidence alone can point to a family on holiday. Add the lack of activity in the house, the milkman doesn't deliver, no children are playing in the garden, and you begin to see that it is quite difficult to hide your absence. It might take people a few days to notice, but the evidence builds up to a point where everyone realizes you are away.

Garden – countermeasures

✓ Water hanging baskets and borders before you go away so that they don't wilt and die.

✓ Cut the lawn, trim the hedge hard and weed the borders.

✓ Give the lawn and hedge an extra trim, the day before you go. Pull out the weeds and water the garden thoroughly to delay the unkempt appearance.

✓ Arrange for a friend or relative to enter the house and make it look lived in for a few hours every now and then. I know a lady who arranges for her neighbour to visit a couple of times a week to tend to the house plants, then to watch television for a few hours, so that people can see activity in the house.

✓ If you have children, you may ask your visiting friend or relative to move a few odd toys around in the garden. They should do this while watering the garden or mowing the grass to make it look innocent. If you leave some toys outside in one place for a couple of weeks this may be noticed. Moving them makes the place look lived in. (Don't leave expensive toys/ bikes outside. 'Dress' your garden with older, less valuable items.)

✓ Check that sheds and garages are locked, cars are in garages with secondary security devices fitted.

✓ Make sure that all ladders, tools and any equipment that could be stolen or used to break into your home are securely locked away.

Dustbin/rubbish collection

Don't forget the dustman. In your first week away you will have rubbish in your bin. Don't leave your bin out in the street ready for emptying, before you go away. It could remain there for the full two weeks of your holiday, advertising to everyone that you are away.

Dustbin/visiting friend or relative – countermeasures

✓ Make things appear as normal as possible to passing criminals, including asking a friendly neighbour or relative to put your bin out and take it in as usual. (You could offer to do the same for your neighbours/friends when they are away.)

✓ Your relative or neighbour should visit your house every day to take junk mail off the step, look after the garden and generally make the house appear to be in use.

✓ Ideally, your friend or relative should spend an hour or so at your house, following the normal pattern of your family. The dustbin should be put out and taken in, following your normal pattern as closely as possible. If it is usually put out the night before, then the neighbour should do the same while you are away. If it is emptied and taken in about mid afternoon, then try to arrange that your neighbour does the same, to maintain a normal appearance. Just like milk piled up on a doorstep, or mail overflowing from a letterbox, an empty dustbin left out overnight is a clear sign that nobody is at home. A burglar will soon notice that and investigate further.

Don't give information away

You have made your house and property as secure as you can and your car is locked away and secure in the garage. Will you damage your security by telling the local criminals that you will be on a beach in Barbados for a couple of weeks? OK, you say you won't, but are you *sure*?

Can you trust everyone who knows you are going on holiday, and the people they will tell? Take a moment to consider how many people may know about your proposed holiday plans.

■ You told the milkman when you cancelled the milk, he was impressed and told everyone at the depot and some of them told their friends and family (total 45 strangers know).

▦ You told the newsagent so their staff and families know. While you told the newsagent there were three other people in the shop at the time and they all told their friends and family (total 75).

▦ The travel agent and staff know, of course, plus anyone they told and anyone else who was in the shop at the time (total 100).

▦ The bank employees know, from when you ordered your US dollars (total 130).

▦ The doctor and his staff know, from when you asked about vaccinations (total 155).

▦ Everyone where you work knows, plus at least a few customers and suppliers (total 220).

▦ Everyone at the local pub and anyone they speak to now know (total 260).

▦ Everyone at Ace Taxis knows, and they even know the dates, times and flight numbers of your departure and return (total 295).

So, without too much trouble we have identified at least a couple of hundred people who could know that you will be out of the country for two weeks, from the 14th. Are you happy with that?

It is incredibly easy for information about your holiday absence to get into the wrong hands, but what can you do about it?

Information – countermeasures

✓   Limit the number of people who know about your holiday. There will be plenty of boasting time when you come back, with loads of holiday snaps and that tasteful straw donkey!

✓   If possible, ask a relative to take you to the airport and collect you on your return, then you won't have to tell any taxi drivers.

✓   If you use a taxi, don't tell them how long you will be gone. Use a different taxi company to collect you on your return. That way nobody knows how long you will be away, Alternatively, ask a relative to book your return taxi a day or so ahead, to protect the information.

✓   I talk to taxi drivers about the weather and traffic, and avoid talking about my plans. They may just be talkative or they may be pumping me for details that I don't really want them to have.

✓   Consider doing some acting! Don't go over the top, but make the taxi driver think there is somebody still at home when you leave. Just as the driver is moving off and can't pay too much attention to the house, wave at your house and say something like, 'Gosh, I didn't think Frank was ever going to let us go.' Do and say just enough to make the taxi driver think that there is somebody still living in your house.

✓   Don't put your home address on your outbound luggage tickets. Anyone at the airport can see that you are going abroad so burglars can treat the departure lounge as a pick-and-mix burglary counter. Criminals can read you! Expensive luggage, booked on the scheduled flight to Barbados, home in the posh district of Commuterville – it won't take them long to spot the worthwhile targets.

✓ Have two luggage tickets, the outward ticket showing your holiday hotel address, and the ticket you put on before coming home again, showing your home address.

House-sitters

Pets have to be considered when you are taking a holiday. Some people can afford to pay for boarding kennels, others have the double benefit of a house-sitter who takes care of their house and their pets. You must be sure that any house-sitter is trustworthy and will maintain security while you are away.

House-sitters – countermeasures

✓ A house will be a lot more secure while you are away if somebody trustworthy is living there.

✓ You can hire a house-sitter, but I would only ask a trusted relative to be a house-sitter.

✓ If you have pets, a house/pet-sitter can be a good idea. Getting a young relative from another part of the country to do it gives them a cheap holiday, you avoid paying expensive kennel fees, your pet stays in familiar surroundings, and your house is occupied and protected.

✓ Train your house-sitter to maintain security, to set the alarm, to work the exterior floodlights etc.

Create an illusion of activity

If your house is left empty, do anything to add to the illusion of life and activity. Use some of my examples or add a few illusions of your own.

Illusion of activity – countermeasures

✓ Possibly invite neighbours to park a car in your drive or outside your house occasionally, to increase the illusion of activity.

✓ If it is safe and appropriate, arrange for neighbours children to play in your garden occasionally, or ask your visiting gardener, or your visiting relative who collects mail and checks the house, to bring their children with them to boost the illusion of occupancy.

✓ You could try carefully rationed acting again. Maybe, when he is leaving, your gardener could stand at the gate and return an 'answer' to an imaginary occupant of the house: 'I'll check to see if I can get a couple of those roses. See you next week.' Keep it low key and only try it once while you are away.

Careful departure

Think security in everything you do. It is pointless taking security measures to make people think you are still at home, if you make so much noise and fuss about leaving that half the county knows that you just left for the airport with three large suitcases.

Leave quietly and, if possible, get a relative to reverse up your drive to your door and slip the cases into the boot with as few people seeing them as possible. If you are going by taxi, arrange to leave at a quiet time of day; don't go at rush hour when half the town will see you loading your cases into the car.

General holiday security advice

For your peace of mind, if nothing else, define a routine for closing the house before you leave. At the airport, or sitting in Aztec ruins in the Andes, you don't want to be worrying about whether you put the cat out, or if anyone actually shut the back door when Uncle George took you to the airport.

Define a procedure, list or method that will take you from room to room, to secure the house, switch on the electric timers, close the bedroom windows, lock the side gate etc.

General holiday security advice – countermeasures

✓ Pay particular attention to securing the house when you are leaving for more than a few hours, particularly when you are going on holiday.

✓ If a friend or relative will be checking your house make sure that they know how to secure the house properly. I attended a burgled house where the burglar had entered through an unlocked rear door. While visiting to check the house, a neighbour had been unable to lock the door so had left it unlocked. The owner hadn't explained the 'knack' of locking that particular door. Worse still, the insurance company refused to pay out because the house was insecure.

Long holidays and business trips

You can cover absences on holidays that last a couple of weeks, but longer holidays and business trips present some unique problems.

I attended a detached house set in large gardens that had been burgled and heavily vandalized. The owners were on a six-month business trip to the USA. Though they had done what they could to disguise their absence, they hadn't planned for the problems a longer absence would cause.

After a couple of months, louts realized the house was unoccupied. They broke in, stole some property and stayed to trash the place. Toilets and basins were broken, taps were left on, paint thrown around and doors ripped off their hinges. The final bill for damage and loss ran to thousands of pounds.

From the road outside the signs and evidence that the house was empty were clear and easy to see.

■ Tall weeds were growing through the drive and around the gates, making it clear the drive and gates were not being used.

■ Bushes in the front garden had grown quickly, partly blocking the front path, the lounge windows and the front doorstep.

■ Ivy on the side of the house had started growing across the living room window at the front of the house.

■ A telephone directory had been delivered and left on the front doorstep, but rain had begun to turn it into paper mulch.

■ The front windows, front door and doorstep were all dirty and dusty, a clear sign that nobody was there.

Overall the impression was of an unloved and unused house, and the yobs spotted it and took advantage of it.

Long holidays and business trips – countermeasures

Take time to identify vulnerabilities unique to your house, then take steps to overcome them.

✓ If you are going away for more than a couple of weeks you MUST have somebody trustworthy looking after your house, performing checks and maintenance duties.

✓ Check your house insurance, some policies are void if the house is empty for more than a specified number of weeks.

✓ Plan around the season during which you will be absent and take steps to overcome any problems.

  • In spring – plants put on a spurt of growth. Arrange for somebody to keep the garden tidy.

  • In summer – drought kills plants, and wasps and other pests build nests and take properties over. Arrange for somebody to be watching for these problems and dealing with them.

  • In autumn – falling leaves are the biggest problem, especially if your garden is usually immaculate. Add a little wind and leaves will collect in sheltered corners, showing that nobody is coming and going, and even causing a fire hazard. Make sure they are raked up and disposed of.

- In winter – the lack of tyre tracks and footprints in frost and snow clearly shows that there is no activity in a house. Arrange for the person visiting your house to drive in and make tyre tracks, clear the path of snow and, after fresh snow, walk up and down the paths to make it look as though there is some life at the house.
- Ask your visiting friend or relative to open and close the gates, shed and garage doors. This sweeps leaves and snow aside, showing that the doors and gates are in use.

✓ Ask the person looking after your house to sweep the path and drive. This will take some time but will show activity and occupation in a number of ways.

✓ Ask them to keep the windows and the front door and doorstep clean to maintain the lived-in look. Remember, all a criminal has to do to see if anyone is at home is to walk up to the front door and ring the bell. Don't give him an excuse or reason to try that.

✓ In the summer and autumn, ask the person looking after your home to check any fruit or vegetables growing in the garden. Easily visible ripening and uncollected fruit is suspicious, so tell them to take it and use it with your blessing.

✓ At Christmas, you might ask them to put up a few decorations so that they can be seen through the front window. Nothing elaborate, just enough to indicate a family at home over Christmas. Just as importantly, they must be taken down at the right time too!

✓ Increasingly, properties need protection at Halloween. British louts' approach to 'trick or treating' is more akin to blackmail than childish fun. I have seen windows broken, cars vandalized and paint thrown over a front door. If you will be away during Hallowe'en arrange for somebody to stay in your house and distribute a few pounds' worth of chocolate and fizzy drink cans to avoid trouble.

✓ Plan to avoid known local problems, such as annual pop festivals or other events that attract large crowds. If there is such a local event, if you can't be at home to protect your property, arrange for somebody to be there to protect it for you!

4

Good Neighbours are an Asset

Everybody has neighbours. They may be inches away behind a party wall, above you in another concrete box council flat, or in the next country mansion three miles away. Your neighbour may be a single person, a family, an office building, a church yard, a motorway junction or anything else.

A good neighbour will improve your security. Residents in a semi-detached house that has a 24-hour petrol station as an immediate neighbour may complain about the constant noise, and the fact that it gives strangers an excuse to be near your house. But think of it another way. There are staff and customers moving around 24 hours a day, watching over your property. A neighbour can be a security threat but can deliver security benefits as well.

From individual neighbourly concerns for people living close by, to more formalized community watch systems, neighbours have co-operated to improve security in an area.

The obvious benefit of getting on with your neighbours is greater security, so take time to make contact with your neighbours.

5

Threats from Bogus Callers

Getting into a house without being seen, finding the valuables and getting out again without being caught can make stealing things quite difficult. Wouldn't it be good if criminals could get you to invite them in, give them some time to look around and then show them out and wave goodbye? Good for them, that is – not good for you!

Some criminals manage to achieve just that. They arrive claiming to have official standing, talk you into letting them in, then trick you into leaving them alone for a while so they can steal things. This is sometimes called a 'distraction burglary'.

Two of them working together find it easier to distract you. For example, a bogus meter reader will ask you to hold his torch while he records the reading. His colleague, who was introduced as a trainee meter reader, has asked if he could use the toilet. While you are holding the torch in the hall, the trainee is searching and stealing from other rooms in the house.

Bogus callers could potentially affect anyone, but is likely to have more serious consequences for the elderly and infirm. They come in many guises; the only effective countermeasure is not to let them into your home.

In a single year 400,000 cases of bogus callers were reported. In about 35% of those cases, the bogus callers managed to get in and steal money or property. Note that this is only 'reported' crime; unreported crime is thought to be at least equal to reported crime, meaning that there could be up to one million cases each year.

Bogus caller – countermeasures

The countermeasures are generally common to all bogus callers.

✓ All officials should carry identification. If they arrive at your front door, ask to see their identification and check it thoroughly before considering letting them in.

✓ Some visitors, like council employees, probably wear a uniform as well, but don't assume anyone in a uniform is trustworthy.

✓ Some visitors may arrive in an official vehicle – don't assume that because he is in a gas company van he is genuine – he may have stolen it!

✓ If you have any doubts, check the phone book to find a number to call to check on the credentials of the man (or woman) on your doorstep.

✓ Never check a visitor's credentials by calling a number they give you; that number may be their crooked accomplice who will of course vouch for them. If you are in any doubt and cannot find a number for the electricity company etc., call the police.

✓ If the caller is genuine, he or she won't mind waiting outside the front door for you to confirm their identity.

✓ Fit and use a door chain, that stops them pushing the door open and coming in uninvited.

✓ If you allow a visitor into your home, never leave them unattended. Stay with them, and if you have any doubts, ask them to leave. If there are two of them you can politely ask one to stay outside as you let the other in; if they are genuine they will not object.

✓ If you are expecting any visitors, make sure that you don't put unnecessary temptations before them. Lock cash and jewellery, etc. out of sight. This isn't an insult to the tradesman or caller, you are simply avoiding mistakes and misunderstandings.

✓ If you have any suspicions at all, call the police and explain the circumstances. They will check with the company or authority to see if they have staff in the area, and dispatch a police officer to check that caller.

✓ Beware of doing business with a door-to-door salesman, builder, gardener or any other tradesman. If you have not asked them to call on you, tell them no thanks and ask them to leave. If they won't go, call the police.

✓ If you do need work done ask friends, family and neighbours to recommend a reliable, trustworthy tradesman who does good work for a fair price.

✓ Get at least three quotes for the work and tell them you are getting three quotes. Arrange for somebody to be with you when they come to do the quote, and stay with them at all times.

✓ Before doing business with anyone check their address. Cowboy tradesmen often advertise with just a mobile number for a contact. If that is all they are willing to give you, say no thanks! If a tradesman gives an address, before agreeing to give them the work, visit the address to make sure they are actually based there in case things go wrong.

✓ Get a schedule of work with the quote: when they will start and when the job will be finished. If you get a vague 'Should take a couple of days and I think I can start next week' say no.

✓ Check their references which should preferably be from local people you know, or can visit, to check on the tradesman and his work.

✓ Do an internet search on the people or companies; there may be good or bad news stories about them.

✓ NEVER pay until you are absolutely and completely happy that the work is completed and that they have done a good job.

✓ Beware of workmen who ask for money up front – too often that trick is used to part you from your money. I won't use a workman who wants any money in advance.

✓ Never buy anything on your doorstep. Their claims are often false, and chances are you will never see them again. It is too great a risk to take.

✓ Sales people are practised at getting your sympathy as a recognized pressure sales technique. If they start looking for sympathy, such as saying he will get the sack if he doesn't make a sale today, ask him to leave.

✓ Even staff of reputable companies can try to wear you down. When you have had enough, be blunt – be rude if you have to – tell them to leave.

✓ The best countermeasure of all is don't open the door, and don't let them in.

✓ If you suspect that bogus caller criminals are operating in your area, report them to the police before they have a chance to steal from vulnerable people nearby.

✓ If you live near any elderly or infirm people, be neighbourly. If you see strangers on their doorstep, especially if they appear to be trying to talk their way in, take the time to drop by and 'say hello'. If the neighbour introduces you to their nephew 'Hank from America', OK. But they may be glad of the support to get rid of a persistent double-glazing salesman or a criminal trying his luck.

✓ Beware, some fittings and fixtures indicate that a resident is infirm and/or vulnerable, which will make them more likely to be targeted by bogus callers and other criminals. Handrails beside the front door, wheelchair access ramps or perhaps an electric wheelchair and charging point outside a house indicate that at least one resident is disabled or infirm. Similarly, an overgrown garden and poor house maintenance could indicate an infirm, disabled or elderly resident.

If you are suspicious or unhappy about a caller, close the door and call the police. If you report somebody, remember to give appropriate details.

6

If the Worst Happens

There are criminals out there; crime happens, no matter how careful you are. You could be unlucky and find that you are the victim of a crime. If the worst happens, what should you do – and why?

REPORT INCIDENTS TO THE POLICE

If you do have to make a telephone call about a suspicious caller, be ready to give as good a description as you can. If all you can report is 'A guy with black hair', don't expect the police to find him.

To find and question your suspicious character, the police need a better description than that, so they know who to look for while they are driving around or checking via CCTV cameras in the town. The more unique identifiers you can give, the easier it will be to find that person. If you describe a white male, six feet six inches tall, shaved head, white trousers and a dark blue jumper, they have something to work on. It's easy to look for a 'very tall bald guy with white trousers and dark blue jumper'.

When they think they have found him further details will help. Such as, 'He spoke with a Welsh accent and had a little red crest on the left breast of his jumper. He had nicotine stains on the fingers of his left hand, a snake tattoo on the back of his right hand and he presented what looked like a home-made gas company identity card stating he was Frank James – District Assessor.'

That gives the police plenty to work on, and if Mr Frank James really is the District Assessor with the local gas company, he won't mind you being careful. If he isn't, he will wish he hadn't come to your door!

If you are reporting something to the police, or recording an incident in a log, write it down as soon as you can, while it is fresh in your memory. That way names, car registration numbers and other such details don't get lost or confused.

Giving a good description

Depending on the circumstances include:

- sex;
- age;
- height;
- weight/build;
- race/colour;
- hair colour/length/style/ornaments etc.;
- clothing/style/colour/markings etc.;

▨ jewellery;

▨ identifying marks – tattoo/birthmarks/scars etc.;

▨ voice/accent/impediment (stutter);

▨ names used – called himself 'Frank James' – or colleague called him 'Barry' etc.;

▨ anything carried/bag/briefcase/clipboard;

▨ other identifying features, e.g. limp on left leg;

▨ what he said – e.g. claimed to be charity collector;

▨ what did he/they touch/eat/drink etc. (fingerprints and DNA);

▨ did they call on anyone else in the area who could give an independent description to police? 'He called on Mrs Biggins at number 42 before he came to me.'

▨ did they have a vehicle – if so, give its:
   • make;
   • model;
   • colour;
   • age;
   • registration number or partial number;
   • markings, e.g. 'Grabbit & Scarper – Builders' in black lettering on side of light blue van – no phone number shown;
   • other identifying features, e.g. rusty roof rack, broken left headlight etc.;
   • direction of travel if it has left the scene, e.g. 'They turned left on to the A40, heading into town.'

The more detail you can supply, the easier you make it for the police to track down the culprit. You should be using your powers of observation and filing details away in your memory so that you can accurately report them later.

If you call the police to report a crime, ask if anyone will be coming to look for fingerprints or other evidence. Tell the police what you have found in your home and ask them when somebody will come. If your house has been burgled or vandalized you don't want to leave broken glass in the kitchen for a week.

If they say an expert will not be visiting you until after the weekend, for instance, explain your circumstances. It may not matter, or you may have to tidy up in order to shut the back door, or get a window boarded up or repaired, or you may need to tidy the bedroom so that you can go to bed. Whatever the circumstances, explain them to the police.

Try to Protect, Record, Search and Detail evidence of a crime.

Protect

The police may send a fingerprint expert around to your home. If a suspicious caller has entered your home you will know what the criminal touched, so you should make a note of that, and protect any surfaces that may still contain his or her fingerprints. For example, they took a bite out of a biscuit while they were there or touched the glass shelf in the kitchen. Tell that to the police and don't touch it until the police have checked it.

Record

The police are often very busy, so there may be nobody free to talk to you until later that day. Any victim should sit and write down as much as they can remember while it is fresh in their mind. Record the details of any known offender, and make a quick note of what they did, from the time they came in to the time they left. What did they say? What did they touch? Did they sneeze into a tissue and then throw it into the bin? Make a note of everything before you forget. DON'T touch anything until the police have had a chance to look at it. They have skills and experience that you don't have, and while there may be no clues in the untidy heap on the living room carpet, you don't want to lose them by being tidy!

If your suspicious caller left through the back door, walked through the flowerbed and jumped over the back fence, take a look without disturbing things. If there is a set of footprints in the rose border, point them out to the police when they come. If it is coming on to rain and you don't know when the police will arrive, consider protecting the footprints if you can. A dustbin lid or a sheet of plastic will protect the print from the rain, as long as you are careful not to damage the prints while you are doing it.

Search

You have given the police as much information about the criminal as you can. Grandfather's antique gold pocket watch is missing, but is that all; did the criminal take anything else? Without disturbing evidence, check to see if anything else is or could be missing. Where did the criminal go, what did he or she have access to? They didn't go near the back bedroom so your savings are safe in the wardrobe. They were alone in the kitchen so ask the policeman to check if the criminal moved the blue glass vase and took the cash box hidden behind it in the cupboard.

Details

We can help the police by digging out more information if we can do so without disturbing evidence.

It will help if we can give the police pictures of Grandfather's antique gold watch, as well as the serial numbers and valuations. All of that will make it easier to find the culprit and the missing items.

DISCOVERING AN INTRUDER

Many burglars won't enter a house when the owner is at home. Occasionally they make mistakes and people have been woken by the sound of an intruder, even during the day. If you disturb an intruder all they will want to do is to get out and get away.

Never attempt to challenge, detain or capture an intruder; you don't know what state of mind they are in. They might even be scared enough to use the screwdriver they used to break open your window as a weapon. Let them go.

Discovering an intruder – countermeasures

✓   Don't try to catch them or see them.

✓   Make as much noise as you can. Shout, use a mobile phone to call the police, make any noise. If there is an intruder, they will run. (The first thing a burglar usually does after entering any premises is to secure his exit route by opening the front or back door etc.).

✓ At the first sign of disturbance they will run and you will be safe.

✓ Prepare to be a little embarrassed. Nine times out of ten, the 'late night intruder' will be your cat coming in for a sleep, water pipes creaking, your teenagers coming in late or somebody getting up for a midnight snack.

COMING HOME TO AN INTRUDER

If you come home to find the front door is open and, even more rarely, there is somebody moving around upstairs using a torch to search for valuables, don't challenge them. Take this advice.

Coming home to an intruder – countermeasures

✓ Don't disturb them or warn them of your presence.

✓ Stay back and out of sight if you can, use a mobile phone to call the police.

✓ Explain that you have returned home to find that intruders are still on the premises.

✓ Pass on any additional information you have. Did you see two people in the house, or a strange white van parked outside your house? Give all the information you have to the police. Try to stay on the line to give a commentary on what is happening. Stay back and stay safe.

GET A POLICE CRIME REFERENCE NUMBER

When you report a crime to the police they usually take the details and give you a reference number that relates to that crime report, but they may call it something different. If they do give you a crime reference number make a note of it because you will need it, especially if you are making a claim on your insurance. If they don't give you a reference number ask for one.

PROTECT, RECORD, SEARCH, AND DETAIL
EVIDENCE OF THE CRIME

To sum up, if there has been a crime, protect the rest of your valuables and any evidence there may be. Record everything you know as soon as you can, before you forget details. Search, as far as you can without disturbing evidence, to see what else has been disturbed and/or taken. Produce as much detail as you can for the police, including descriptions of people, make, model, serial number and photographs of stolen property. All of this will be very helpful in tracing the property and identifying the criminal.

CLAIMING OFF YOUR INSURANCE

If you have insurance, contact the insurance company to report the crime and make a claim. If you make a claim before you have had time to undertake a thorough search, report everything that has been stolen, but tell them that there could be other things that you may wish to add later.

Most insurance companies require you to give them a relevant police crime reference number. Some stipulate that unless you report the crime to the police and receive a crime reference number, you wont be able to claim on your insurance.

REVIEWING YOUR SECURITY AFTER A CRIME

Perhaps the burglar just used a paving slab to smash the glass in your patio door, but he may have found a weakness in your security. Whatever the circumstances, you must perform an immediate security review to identify vulnerabilities and implement countermeasures where possible to prevent any further loss.

Don't make your house too secure. Sometimes people react to crime by introducing ultra high security, triple locking and bolting all of the doors and putting steel bars on the windows. Nobody wants to live in a fortress, and remember, you need to be able to get out quickly if there is a fire, so only take 'reasonable countermeasures'.

RECLAIMING YOUR HOME AFTER A CRIME

Your home is your private domain, a place where you should be able to relax and feel safe. Many people feel that a burglary or other criminal intrusion damages or destroys that feeling of safety and security. In their mind the home feels corrupted and sullied because the criminal has violated their space.

Some people feel strongly that happy family memories are overwritten by the burglary, and missing items and broken windows constantly remind them of the intruder. Women often experience revulsion and fear more than men, and that 'bad feeling' causes additional stress to the family after the crime.

Though it will fade over time, it is distressing and damaging to family life. However, these feelings can be erased, overwritten, washed away or counterbalanced with 'good memories'. Victims of intruder crimes have found that the following measures have helped to make their house feel like home again.

Fix the problem – countermeasures

✓ First, and most importantly, find out how the criminal overcame your security and take steps to stop it happening again. You will sleep easier knowing that your security is tight again.

Refresh or remove – countermeasures

✓ Where possible and affordable, dispose of anything that has been sullied by the touch of the criminal. (I remember a lady who refused to wear any of her clothes because the burglar had searched through her clothes looking for valuables.)

✓ If furniture is involved, you can swap a 'tainted' dressing table that the burglar looked through with a similar one at a second-hand shop for a modest fee, or swap it with a relative!

✓ Brand new bed sheets really feel 'clean and new' if you can afford to buy them. Get a similar relief by swapping bedding and curtains with relatives.

✓   It may be possible to professionally clean an item that has been corrupted by an intruder; for example, have the carpets professionally cleaned to remove all traces of the villain. The basic rule is to take any steps you can to refresh your home.

Decorate – countermeasures

✓   Some people sense the 'smell' and 'feel' of the criminal's presence constantly. Redecorating gives the house a fresh new look, and helps by distancing the current home from the home that was violated by an intruder.

Party – countermeasures

✓   After taking as many steps as are practical and affordable to you, you should have a party for as many good friends and relatives as you can. Warn them that any discussion or questions about the crime will destroy what you have been trying to achieve. Make this the happiest party ever, flooding the 'new look' home with new happy memories revolving around friends, fun and a good time.

Combination – countermeasures

✓   I knew a lady who was so traumatized by a burglary that she wanted to sell up and move out. Her husband arranged for her to stay with their daughter for a holiday. While she was away, he installed new door and window locks, a burglar alarm, and passive sensor-operated lighting on the sides and rear of the house. He also decorated throughout and upgraded the kitchen. The lady came home to a big party and said it was like coming into a new house.

Hopefully, all of those actions will make the home feel like a safe shelter from the world again. Remember, children may be traumatized too! After talking things through sensibly, and listing the new security measures that you have taken to make the house even safer, stop talking about the crime and do anything you can to help yourself and your family to rebuild the feeling of security that they need.

7

Implementing Your Chosen Countermeasures

When you have completed your home security survey, what should you do? This chapter suggests a simple approach to selecting, documenting and implementing your countermeasures.

IDENTIFYING SECURITY ISSUES

You have probably already started responding to and resolving some of the problems you identified. The next step is to formally manage and resolve the outstanding problems by implementing appropriate countermeasures.

During the survey you may have simply listed problems and appropriate countermeasures, or you may have added pages of notes. Some countermeasures may have been so simple that you have already carried them out, such as shutting the utility room window instead of leaving it open for the cat. Other problems and countermeasures are waiting your attention. Your next task is to decide what to implement, how, and in what order, to do it.

LISTING PROBLEMS AND COUNTERMEASURES

From the notes you took during the security review, draw up a tidy list of all of the problems you identified.

Against each problem, list any appropriate countermeasures. There may be problems for which you have not yet identified possible countermeasures. If so, list them without countermeasures.

The problems you identify may be quite lengthy, for example 'Front door swells up and sticks in winter, but dries out and shrinks in summer, making the front door loose and insecure or too stiff to open.' Assign each problem with a number and key word.

Ref No	Key Word	Problem	Countermeasure	Priority
SRI/I	Porch	It is possible for intruders to hide in porch alcove.	Fit door viewer in front door and fit light on porch.	
SRI/2	Front door	Front door swells up and sticks in winter, but dries out and shrinks in summer, making the front door loose and insecure.	Fit new door and frame with security equipment identified in SRI/3, SRI/4 and SRI/5 below.	
SRI/3	Front door	Letterbox unprotected.	Fit draught excluder and mail basket inside letterbox.	
SRI/4	Front door	No hinge bolts on front door.	Fit hinge bolts.	
SRI/5	Front door	No approved mortice lock on front door.	Fit approved mortice lock.	

Identify and select countermeasures

Take some time to review and research the countermeasures. This allows you to select and list those that you will implement. Research may include the following:

- Seek expert advice – which locks are best for a patio door or a garage?

- Investigate the need for planning permission to erect a wall or fence.

- Seek permission for structural changes from your landlord.

- Look into the availability and cost of new fixtures and fittings.

- Investigate availability, time, skills, tools and costs involved in implementing specific countermeasure.

- Seek advice from police, they may suggest countermeasures where you could not identify one.

This should help you to select the countermeasures you want to introduce to improve your security and to compile a final list of all identified problems and proposed countermeasures.

Establish countermeasure priority

Using Post-it notes or slips of paper, sort them into order of priority, under four main headings:

- (I) IMMEDIATE;

- (S) SOON;

■   (I and W) IF AND WHEN POSSIBLE;

■   (NS) NON-SECURITY.

Write the reference number and key word of each problem and the countermeasures on a new Post-it note and add them to the appropriate list.

Thus you might write 'SR1/1 Porch – fit porch light' and on another Post-it note, 'SR1/1 Porch – fit door viewer'. Using the reference number and key word makes the task manageable, and what you write is enough to remind you what it is.

Using your perception of the priority, time required, cost, skills, impact and benefit, produce a final countermeasure priority list. Remember that the priority rating you assign to each one will be a combination of factors, the most important of which are:

■   the threat or risk that the countermeasure will remove or protect against. A rotten front door to which you lost two keys with address tags is a major concern. The door is no longer secure at all;

■   the time required to implement the countermeasure. Replacing the front door will take about half a day;

■   the cost of implementing the countermeasure. A total of £418 is quite expensive, but a secure front door is so fundamental to the security of your house that it must be done as soon as possible;

▪ the skills needed to implement the countermeasure. A carpenter must fit the door. If you don't have those skills you must hire someone who does;

▪ the impact on your family and your house of implementing the countermeasure. Having no front door for half a day while it is replaced is OK in summer. I can work at home that day so the impact is minimal;

▪ the overall benefits that will be gained by implementing the countermeasure. A professionally installed door, frame and new locks etc. will be totally secure;

▪ the financial benefits of increased security. Insurance companies may reduce insurance premiums when double-glazing and multi-point-locking external doors are fitted.

If you have too many countermeasures to cope with, do the sorting in stages. Take each item and put it into piles: (I) Immediate; (S) Soon; (I and W) If and When Possible; and (NS) Non-security. Then carefully review and sort each problem in each pile separately.

▪ **Immediate** list contains all actions that should be completed urgently, such as replacing that front door. It may include apparently 'non-urgent' items such as that the bushes at the front of the house should be cut back. That is not 'urgent', but it will only take half an hour, it costs nothing and you can do it before it gets dark. You may as well do it now and cross it off the list, so it appears on the immediate list.

▪ **Soon** list contains all actions that should be completed soon, but are not urgent or immediate as such. Examples include replacing the lock on the garage door. The old lock still works at the moment, so you will get a new garage lock next month.

▪ **If and When Possible** list contains actions that deliver 'nice to have' countermeasures, such as a state-of-the-art burglar alarm. It would increase household security immeasurably, but at £3,000 it will just be a 'nice to have' countermeasure.

▪ **Non-Security** list contains those countermeasures not directly related to security, but which you would be foolish to ignore. Examples include a loose slate that you spotted when performing the perimeter survey. You must resolve these, and the non-security list is the mechanism through which you manage them.

Countermeasure prioritization

You must consider all factors in order to prioritize the countermeasures. The process is straightforward, though not necessarily simple. Follow the example below, which illustrates the thoughts and processes in sorting just four countermeasures.

1.   Cut down shrubs in front garden.
2.   Replace broken front door lock.
3.   Renew old front door.
4.   Ensure house always locked when we leave.

See the sample prioritized list below, with explanations to help you understand why I set them in this order.

Prioritized Actions	Explanation as to why the countermeasures were placed in this priority order
I. Everyone to agree to ensure that the house is always locked when we leave.	During the security survey my wife and I realized we are sometimes a little careless about household security — not locking up if we are 'only nipping down to the shops'. We recognized the risk and have already agreed always to lock and secure the house every time we go out. This action was agreed, and completed over breakfast this morning.
2. Cut down shrubs in front garden.	We have avoided tackling the front garden. We didn't think it mattered but we now realize that the overgrown bushes could help burglars to raid our house. The shops are shut so we cannot tackle the other countermeasures. We'll therefore make best use of our time and cut the bushes back now. NOTE: If the shops had been open, this would have been a lower priority, but due to current circumstances it became the highest priority because it is the only countermeasure we can do anything to implement now.
3. Replace broken front door lock.	The front door lock has been temperamental for months, but we put off getting it fixed because we want a new front door. Now we realize that a secure front door is important and as soon as the shops open tomorrow we'll buy and fit a new lock. It won't be a waste because the carpenter says he can use that new lock on the new door when he fits it.
4. Renew old front door.	The current front door is warped and when the wind is from the west it lets rain in. There is some rot at the bottom of the door, but it is adequate for now. I don't have the skills and tools needed to fit a new door, so we will have to pay for a new door to be fitted. John the carpenter says he will do it next month when we can afford it.

It is perfectly acceptable for you to prioritize the countermeasures in a different order. The whole point of this method and process is to tailor the reviews, actions and countermeasures to your personal circumstances.

Revisit and revise your priorities

Your circumstances may change over time, and this may alter the order in which countermeasures are implemented. A new front door is your highest priority so you have one on order, but the earliest delivery is four weeks away. In that case you have time to do some other lower priority tasks. That is acceptable. If you address the items in priority order, resolving them as soon as you can, the order in which they are completed doesn't really matter.

Prioritization considerations

The list below includes issues that may affect your priority decisions. Take a while to think of the other pressures and restrictions that are unique to you.

Considerations	Explanation/examples of why an action may be delayed
Money	If you cannot afford it, it will have to wait.
Time available	If you don't have time, it will have to wait.
Skills/knowledge	If you don't know how to do it, or lack special skills, it will have to wait.
Tools/equipment	If you don't have specialist tools and equipment required, it will have to wait.
Weather/season	You may have to wait for warm dry weather before tackling an exterior task.
Planning rules	You may have to wait for planning permission.
Assistance	You may have to wait until somebody is available to help you.

Keep track of the 'as and when possible' list of countermeasures. They may be beyond your means now, but keep them in mind because your circumstances may change.

DRAWING UP AN ACTION LIST

Implementing one countermeasure may be easy, while implementing another may be a major project. For each countermeasure you may want to list the actions required to implement it. On an action list, the tasks needed are listed in the order in which they need to be completed to deliver the countermeasure.

Of course, if the countermeasure is simple, such as fitting a new bulb in the porch light, you won't bother to create an action list, but where the countermeasure is more complicated an action list will be a huge help.

Example action list

Standardize house identification in our street. For this countermeasure we must look at the actions we will need to complete in order to implement it. The list will show each action needed, in the order in which they must be completed. When finished, the action list also becomes a plan, check-list and work schedule that will help you to introduce that countermeasure.

For this example the action list may consist of the following measures.

- Research availability, style, size and cost of house name signs.

- Research methods of erecting house name signs for optimum visibility.

- Investigate the possibility of discounts if we all buy from the same company.

- Check that the most appropriate sign and mounting system will work on every property in the road.

- Discuss the proposal with emergency services and record their comments.

- Find local handyman who could install all of the signs.

- Make presentation to residents' committee of risks and dangers of emergency services being unable to find any given house. Describe problems when testing finding a house in dark and rain, explain damage and risk to security and health of everyone in the street.

- Make presentation of research into signs. Present samples and costs, noting savings and discounts negotiated. Describe comments from emergency services re standardized sign initiative.

- Request that residents' association vote.

- If accepted, all residents to fill in order form and pay for their sign and erection.

- Take delivery of the new signs and mounting brackets etc.

- Arrange with the handyman to fit all of the signs.

When those steps are completed, the countermeasure has been implemented. *NOTE*: the necessary steps and actions could take some weeks to complete.

Action list considerations

The action list for more complex countermeasures (shown here) also helps you to understand the effort, cost and time required to implement each countermeasure, because it allows you to break down the tasks required into manageable and understandable proportions, arriving at a work schedule, time-scale and cost.

SRI/27 Standardize House Names and Identification For Badger Road					
No.	Action	Cost	Time	Skills	Impact
1.	Research availability, style and cost of house name signs.	Nil	10 days	Internet Phone Directory	Nil
2.	Research mounting and positioning signs for optimum visibility.	Nil	5 days	Advice Police and Builder	Nil
3.	Investigate discounts on bulk orders.	Nil	10 days	Get quotes	Nil
4.	Check that selected option will fit every property in the road.	Nil	1 day	Check each property	Extra work may be required at some houses.
5.	Discuss the proposal with emergency services.	Nil	5 days	Nil	They like the idea and will feature it in newsletters and staff magazines.
6.	Find a local handyman to install signs and negotiate discount.	Nil	5 days	Nil	Nil
7.	Present findings to residents' committee.	Nil	1 hour	Nil	Nil
8.	Present research re signs with samples, mention cost and discounts.	Nil	1 hour	Nil	Nil
9.	Request vote on the initiative.	Nil	10 mins	Nil	Nil or authorization to order the signs and work to begin.
10.	If accepted, issue forms and collect money.	£1 to print forms	15 mins	Nil	Nil
11.	Take delivery of the new signs etc.	Nil	1 day	Nil	Arrange for signs to be delivered to handyman.
12	Arrange for handyman to fit signs.	£10 per house	Nil	Nil	Pay handyman when job inspected and complete.

The example schedule shows that there is almost no cost to implement this countermeasure, other than actually buying the signs and having them erected.

At 37 days, 2 hours and 25 minutes, the time required seems excessive, but as the objective is to make every house in the street easily identifiable, a lead time of a month or so is quite acceptable. But if we take a closer look at the time required, we can see that it may not take a month.

■ Most of the time allocated is for research as a background task for one resident, and it includes waiting time for quotes to come through the post.

■ Look at the sequence too.
  • Action 1 – research availability and cost of signs.
  • Action 2 – research method of erecting those signs. So actions 1 and 2 can possibly be run in parallel.
  • Action 3 – research possible discounts, which can probably be done on first contact, so action 3 can run in parallel with actions 1 and 2.
  • Action 4 – check the option will work on all houses. Though listed to take a day, this can be done quite early in the process and could be completed before actions 1, 2, and 3 are completed, so they will all run in parallel.
  • Action 5 – consult emergency services. We can easily talk about what we are planning, and anything that helps them will no doubt be popular.
  • Actions 7, 8, 9 and 10 take only a short time at the next residents' association meeting.
  • Action 11 takes one day because the company offers next-day delivery!

- Though the total time added up to 37 days, 2 hours and 25 minutes, in reality – with a bit of luck – the handyman can start putting the new signs up within a couple of weeks!

▤ No special skills are required, with no real impact.

▤ The details for each action could include:
  - Time – how long (measured in hours) will it take.
  - Cost – how much will it cost to do it?
  - Skills – any special skills required.
  - Impacts – you must decide what, if any, impacts the countermeasure will have. You could perhaps find that to erect the new sign the handyman has to turn off the electricity in your house for a short while.

Here is an additional sample action list.

Badger View – 'new front door' action list

Countermeasure	Actions	Priority
Fit new front door Time – 4 hrs for carpenter to install it. Cost – £145 for door, £78 for door furniture; preparation and labour, £195. Skills – carpenter with experience of locks and other security devices. Impact – door will be removed for 4 hours, somebody will have to be at home that day.	1. Speak to carpenter and explain requirement. 2. Select door from range carpenter has available. 3. With advice from carpenter select locks and security devices. 4. Select other door furniture. 5. Check, approve and accept final total cost. 6. Arrange date for work to be done. Book that day off work. 7. Remove keys and furniture from front hall so carpenter has room to work. 8. Watch carpenter to confirm he is doing what was asked and make sure nobody sneaks into house while front door is removed.	IMMEDIATE The existing front door is rotten, the frame is loose and two front door keys cannot be found.

Badger View – non-security 'loft plumbing' action list

Countermeasure	Actions	Priority
Lag pipes in loft Time – 1 hour. Cost – £12 to buy lagging material. Skills – none needed. Impact – none.	1. Buy DIY pack of pipe lagging. 2. Fit lagging to the pipes that are not lagged.	IMMEDIATE It is autumn, long-range forecasts predict very cold weather next month. It would be foolish not to do the job this weekend.

GUARDING AGAINST ACCIDENTS AT HOME

Security is the application of methods and procedures used to make our lifestyle secure against any vulnerabilities, threats and risks. By applying security appropriately, we will maximize safety.

Accidents are a threat to our safety and security, so we will take a brief look at accident prevention in the home. Most injuries are caused by accidents inside the home, resulting in injuries and fatalities.

Some if the most common accidents are the following.

■ **Falls/slips/trips** Causes include loose carpet; toys left on stairs and steps; trailing wires and loose floorboards etc; using inappropriate items to climb to reach high objects (climbing on furniture instead of using a ladder); small dogs (tripping elderly people); and wet floors/oil spillage etc.

- **Burns/scalds** Causes include spills or misuse of boiling water; food (hot drinks and soup), cooking oil; household chemicals (bleach and other caustic materials); hot utensils (burns from cooking dishes) etc.

- **Poisoning** Causes include gas (faulty gas appliances/blocked air vents/faulty devices/poor installation and maintenance); misuse of household and garden chemicals (child drinks weedkiller kept in lemonade bottle) etc.

- **Cuts** Includes cuts from broken glass; misuse of knives and tools (using a knife as a screwdriver); and carelessness (cutting your hand as you open a baked bean tin) etc.

- **Electrocution** Often caused by unskilled people attempting to repair a vacuum cleaner or other faulty device, and unskilled attempts to install or amend electrical wiring.

- **Explosions** Caused by misuse of gas and/or flammable fluids, such as naked flame exposed to gas leak, or perhaps careless storage and use of petrol.

- **Fire** Can be caused by some of the above behaviour and activity, careless disposal of cigarettes; carelessness in the use of gas and electric fires; paraffin heaters; or lack of care when burning rubbish or letting off fireworks.

- **Machinery injury** Often caused by misuse of garden equipment (lawn mowers, hedge trimmers, chain-saws), vehicles, kitchen equipment (blenders, waste disposal units), electrical tools (drills, planes or disc cutters).

■ **Combination** Any of the above causes could act in combination, for example misuse of electric drill causing fuel to leak which causes fire and explosion.

Accidents at home – countermeasures

Don't make your home as secure from crime as you can and then allow yourself and family members to be injured or killed by careless accidents.

✓ Use or wear recommended safety equipment, safety glasses, gloves and steel-toed boots etc.

✓ Read, understand and follow carefully all instructions for any tool or equipment.

✓ Use safety guards and equipment at all times.

✓ If you are unsure or have any safety concerns, stop what you are doing. Seek advice, guidance and/or training.

✓ Keep your working area clear of obstructions or hazards before beginning work.

✓ Take all safety measures seriously and never take shortcuts.

✓ Always keep tools and equipment in perfect working order and check them before using them.

✓ Warn anyone else when you are about to start a job, and if necessary erect protective barriers.

✓ Before you begin any job, take some time first to consider and assess the risk and to get everything ready before you start.

✓ As a general rule, make sure that your living and working areas are clean, clear and tidy.

Useful websites

Security is largely a question of awareness and common sense, so access to the Internet is not essential. However, the Internet does make a world of information available to everyone.

Some people may feel excluded because they do not have a home computer or advanced computer skills, but they are not necessary. You can use the Internet in coffee shops, libraries, colleges and schools and there is usually somebody available to show you how to use it too. By the time the average person has had a little practice, they usually say that they don't know why they were so nervous in the first place!

Below I have listed some of the most useful Internet sites relevant to ensuring the security of your home.

Flooding Information Environment Agency

www.environment-agency.gov.uk Type in your postcode to identify the flooding risk for any location and property.

Crime statistics

www.crimestatistics.org.uk Allows you to check crime figures for a specific area. Some local authorities also hold information about crime rates and trends.

Stolen property searches

The police have their own database which is not available to the public, but there are also some databases that are available for the public to use.

www.trace.co.uk

www.virtualbumblebee.co.uk

Stopping unwanted mail, fax and phone advertising

If you want to try to stop, or at least reduce, the amount of unsolicited advertising you receive by mail, fax and telephone sent from UK organizations, visit the following specific sites to register your details. It will take a few months to work and isn't guaranteed to stop all junk mail, but it helps.

www.fpsonline.org.uk Register your number and state that you do not want unsolicited fax advertising material.

www.mpsonline.org.uk Register your number and state that you do not want unsolicited mail advertising material.

www.tpsonline.org.uk Register your number and state that you do not want unsolicited telephone advertising material.

Index